I0605227

CHURCHILL

AND THE GENERALS

Mike Lepine

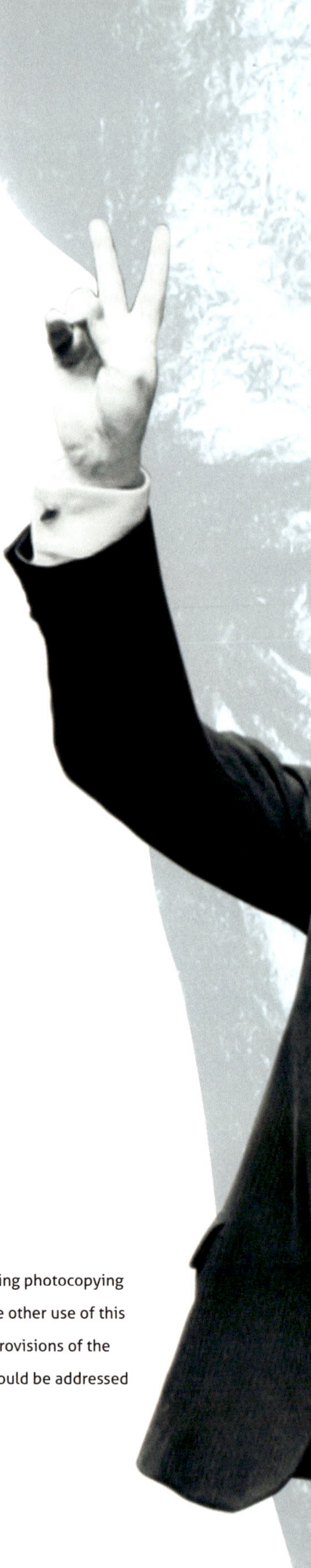

First Published Danann Publishing Ltd 2015

CAT NO: SON0642

Photography courtesy of

BBC
Getty images
Popperfoto/Getty Images
Hulton Archive/Getty Images
Central Press/Getty Images
Keystone/Getty Images
Express/Getty Images
Universal History Archive/UIG via Getty Images

Other images Wiki Commons

Book layout & design Darren Grice at Ctrl-d

Made in EU.

ISBN: 978-1-917259-12-5

CONTENTS

A SELECTIVE WWII CHRONOLOGY 10

WINSTON CHURCHILL .28

BROOKE - THE OTHER HALF. 82

ISMAY - THE RELUCTANT CIVIL SERVANT. 88

MONTGOMERY - THE OUTSIDER 92

IRONSIDE - THE BRUISER 102

WAVELL - THE SCHOLAR. 108

AUCHINLECK - MAN OF EMPIRE 114

ALEXANDER - THE DANDY. 120

DILL - THE BRIDGE-BUILDER. 126

WILSON - THE DEPENDABLE 130

MARSHALL - THE PROFESSIONAL 134

EISENHOWER - THE SPEARHEAD 138

1940: Churchill wears helmet during air raid warning

A SELECTIVE WORLD WAR TWO CHRONOLOGY

1939

SEPTEMBER

1 – Germany invades Poland

1 – Blackout announced in Britain

1 – The British Army is officially mobilised

2 – Neville Chamberlain attempts to negotiate peace between Germany and Poland but is forced by Parliament to issue an ultimatum instead

3 – Britain and France declare war on Germany

3 – First air raid sirens heard in London (False alarm)

3 – Chamberlain establishes his War Cabinet

3 – Australia, New Zealand and India declare war on Germany

3 – Ironside appointed Chief of the Imperial General Staff (CIGS)

3 - Dill appointed Commander, I Corps, BEF

3 – Winston Churchill appointed First Lord of the Admiralty

5 – America announces it will stay neutral

6 – South Africa declares war on Germany

10 – Canada declares war on Germany

17 – The Soviet Union invades Poland

25 – Germany introduces rationing

3rd September 1939: Arriving at the Admiralty, London, at the start of World War II to begin his second term as First Lord of the Admiralty

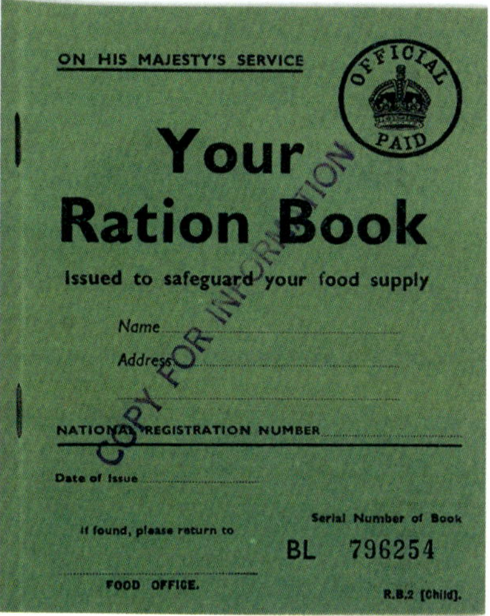

CIRCA 1940: Childs Ration Book

7TH AUGUST 1940: Winston Churchill inspecting Mk II howitzers, during a tour of East Coast defences

CIRCA 1940: Lord Edmund Ironside before being promoted to Field Marshal

1940

OCTOBER

3 – British forces advance to the Belgian border anticipating German attack on France

6 – Hitler makes peace overtures towards France and Britain

10 – Chamberlain rejects Hitler's bid for peace

12 – France rejects Hitler's bid for peace

27 – Belgium announces its neutrality

DECEMBER

2 – British conscription is expanded to include all men between the ages of 19 and 41

18 – First Canadian troops arrive in Britain

JANUARY

8 – Rationing begins in Britain

FEBRUARY

15 – Wavell becomes C-in-C Middle East

APRIL

9 – Germany invades Norway

9 – Germany invades Denmark

9 – Denmark surrenders

14 – British and French troops arrive in Norway

22 – Dill appointed vice-CIGS

27 – British troops begin pull out from Norway

MAY

10 – Germany invades France, Belgium, Luxembourg and the Netherlands; The Blitzkrieg begins

10 – Winston Churchill is appointed as Prime Minister, heading a coalition government

13 – Churchill delivers his 'blood, toil, tears, and sweat' speech to Parliament

14 – Local Defence Volunteers (Later to be called the Home Guard) established by Secretary of State for War Anthony Eden

15 – Holland surrenders

16 – Churchill flies to France and discovers the French Army is in a state of near collapse

23 – British fascist leader Oswald Mosley arrested and jailed

26 – British troops from the BEF begin to evacuate from Dunkirk

27 – Ironside relieved as Chief of the Imperial General Staff (CIGS)

27 – Ironside appointed C-in-C Home Forces

27 – Dill appointed Chief of the Imperial General Staff (CIGS)

28 – Belgium surrenders

CIRCA 1940: Sheet of Wehrmacht 50g bread ration stamps. Nazi Germany

2 posters from the famous "Dig For Victory" campaign

CIRCA 1940: German Sailors Prepare for Operation Sea Lion

CIRCA 1940: Churchill with members of the Anglican clergy through the ruins of Coventry Cathedral

CIRCA 1940: Pilots of No 54 Squadron RAF gathered round a Supermarine Spitfire Mark IIA at Rochford, Kent

JUNE

3 – Last BEF troops evacuated from the beaches of Dunkirk

4 – Churchill makes his famous 'we shall fight them on the beaches' speech

10 – Norway surrenders

10 - Italy declares war on Britain and France

12 – Brooke appointed C-in-C (designate) of the BEF

14 – The Soviet Union begins its annexing of the Baltic States

18 – Churchill gives his 'Finest Hour' speech

19 – Auchinleck appointed GOC-in-C Southern Command

25 – France surrenders

30 – Germany invades the Channel Islands

JULY

2 – Hitler orders preparations for the invasion of Britain (Operation Sea Lion)

10 – Battle of Britain begins

19 – Ironside promoted to Field Marshal

19 – Brooke appointed C-in-C, Home Forces

22 – Montgomery becomes GOC V Corps, England

AUGUST

3 - Italians attack British Somaliland

20 – Churchill delivers 'The Few' speech to parliament

24 – German bomber accidentally bombs London

25/26 – First British bombing raid on Berlin

SEPTEMBER

7 – Blitz on British cities by the Luftwaffe begins

13 – Italian forces invade Egypt

20 – America agrees to supply Britain with 50 destroyers in exchange for base rights in the Caribbean.

OCTOBER

10 – Churchill becomes head of the Conservative Party when Chamberlain resigns for health reasons

12 – Hitler decides to postpone the invasion of Britain until 1941

28 – Italy attacks Greece

NOVEMBER

5 – Roosevelt re-elected for the third time as U.S. President

9 – Neville Chamberlain dies

14 – The Greeks launch a counter-offensive against the invading Italians

19 – British forces in the Sudan attack Italian-occupied Eritrea

21 – Auchinleck relieved as GOC-in-C Southern Command

25 – The Soviet Union applies to join the Axis of Germany and Italy

DECEMBER

1 - U.S. Ambassador to Britain Joseph Kennedy sacked by President Roosevelt after he tells the press that 'Democracy is finished in England.'

9 – British forces attack Italians in the Western Desert

4TH JULY 1941: Churchill and King Peter II of Yugoslavia with Montgomery

CIRCA 1941: German troops in Russia

1941

JANUARY

5 – Australian troops seize 45,000 prisoners at Bardia in Libya

16 – British forces in Kenya attack Italian-held Ethiopia

22 – British forces take port city of Tobruk

FEBRUARY

7 – 130,000 Italians surrender to the Allies at Benghazi

11 – British forces attack Italian Somaliland

14 – First elements of the German Afrika Korps land in North Africa

22 – Wilson appointed Commander of the Greek Expedition

25 – Capital of Italian Somaliland captured by British forces

MARCH

7 – British forces arrive in Greece

8 – Buckingham Palace is struck by bombs during an air raid

11 – America agrees 'Lease-Lend' legislation

APRIL

6 – The Afrika Korps recaptures Benghazi

6 – Germany invades Greece

6 – Germany invades Yugoslavia

10 – Elements of the Afrika Korps advance to the Egyptian border

17 – Yugoslavia surrenders

22 – British forces begin to evacuate from Greece

27 – Greece surrenders

27 – Montgomery becomes GOC XII Corps, England

MAY

6 – Wilson appointed as Commander of British troops in Palestine and Trans-Jordan

15 – British counter-attack in Egypt

20 – German paratroopers attack Crete

28 – British and Commonwealth forces begin to evacuate Crete

JUNE

1 – Clothing rationing introduced in Britain

8 – Allied forces invade Lebanon

8 – Allied forces invade Syria

16 - Operation Battleaxe fails to relieve the siege of Tobruk

22 – Wavell fired as C-in-C Middle East

22 – Wavell appointed as C-in-C India

22 – Germany invades the Soviet Union (Operation Barbarossa)

JULY

5 – Auchinleck assumes role of C-in-C Middle East

12 – Britain and the Soviet Union agree a mutual assistance pact

AUGUST

9 – Churchill and Roosevelt meet in Newfoundland

14 – Britain and the U.S. agree the Atlantic Charter

31ST DECEMBER 1941: German Soldiers enduring a Russian winter

CIRCA 1942: "Avenge December 7!" US Government propaganda poster

23 AUGUST 1942: Churchill with General Harold Alexander and Montgomery, during second visit to the Western Desert

25 – Britain and the Soviet Union launch a joint invasion of Iran to protect oilfields

SEPTEMBER

8 – Siege of Leningrad begins

NOVEMBER

17 - Joseph Grew, the United States Ambassador to Japan, warns that the Japanese are planning an attack on Pearl Harbor. His warning is somehow ignored.

19 – Dill relieved of post of Chief of the Imperial General Staff (CIGS)

DECEMBER

3 - Conscription in Britain extended to all men between the ages of 18 and 50.

6 – Major Soviet counterattack drives the Germans out of the suburbs of Moscow

7 – Japanese aircraft and mini submarines attack Pearl Harbor

7 – Japan attacks British Malaya

7 – Japan attacks Thailand

8 - Britain and the U.S. declare war on Japan

9 – Australia declares war on Japan

11 – Germany and Italy declare war on America

11 – America declares war on Germany and Italy

11 – Japanese forces invade Burma

12 – India declares war on Japan

18 - Hong Kong invaded by the Japanese

19 - Hitler appoints himself Supreme Commander-in-Chief of the German Army

22 - Churchill and Roosevelt meet in Washington DC

25 – Dill promoted to Field Marshal

25 – Allied troops re-take Benghazi

25 – Brooke promoted to Chief of the Imperial General Staff (CIGS)

26 – Churchill addresses the American Congress

Also this month– Wilson appointed as Commander of the 9th Army in Syria and Palestine

1942

JANUARY

3 – Wavell becomes Allied Supreme Commander, South West Pacific (ABDA Command)

21 – Afrika Korps launches a counter offensive

26 – First U.S. forces arrive in Britain

FEBRUARY

15 – Singapore falls to the Japanese

22 - ABDA Command ended. Wavell becomes C-in-C India

MARCH

17 – In Britain, electricity, coal and gas is put on ration

1942: Portrait of Winston Churchill

CIRCA 1942: British Land Army girls and members of the Women's Royal Air Force dance with men of the US Eighth Army Air Force in Suffolk

CIRCA 1942: Messerschmitt Me 262, the world's first jet fighter

MAY

20 – The Japanese complete their conquest of Burma

30 – Britain launches first 'Thousand Bomber Raid' against Cologne

JUNE

18 – Churchill arrives in Washington for talks with Roosevelt

21 – Afrika Korps recapture Tobruk

25 – Eisenhower arrives in London to take up position of Commander of American forces in Europe.

25 – Auchinleck takes personal control of the British 8th Army

JULY

2 - Churchill survives a censure motion in the House of Commons

18 – Germany test flies the first combat jet of World War Two – the Me262

AUGUST

8 – Auchinleck fired as C-in-C Middle East

12 – Churchill meets with Stalin in Moscow

13 – Montgomery assumes command of the British 8th Army

15 - Alexander takes over as Commander-in-Chief Middle East,

19 - Dieppe raid by Canadian and British forces ends in disaster, but valuable lessons are learned for D-Day

21 – Wilson appointed Commander of the 10th Army in Persia and Iraq

SEPTEMBER

2 – Rommel beaten by Montgomery at the Battle of Alam Halfa

13 – The Battle of Stalingrad begins

OCTOBER

23 – Battle of El Alamein commences

NOVEMBER

1 – Montgomery launches Operation Supercharge as the next phase of the Alamein offensive

3 – Allies achieve victory in Battle of El Alamein as Rommel's forces forced to retreat

8 – U.S. invades North Africa (Operation Torch)

10 – Celebrating victory at El Alamein, Churchill declares, 'This is not the end. It is not even the beginning of the end. But it is, perhaps, the end of the beginning.'

10 – Montgomery promoted to full General from Lieutenant General and knighted

11 – Germans invade previously unoccupied 'Vichy' France

13 – British 8th army recaptures Tobruk

20 – British forces recapture Benghazi

1943

JANUARY

1 – Wavell promoted to Field Marshal

3 – Montgomery becomes C-in-C 21st Army Group 14-24 – Casablanca Summit held

CIRCA 1942: The second battle of Libya. Before zero hour. The Brigadier commanding tank units in Tobruk instructing tank commanders on the operations

5TH JUNE 1943: Churchill in Downing Street giving his famous 'V' sign

23 – British 8th Army march into Tripoli

27 - U.S.A.A.F planes bomb Germany for the first time

FEBRUARY

2 – German armies at Stalingrad surrender

11 - Eisenhower is selected to command the Allied armies in Europe.

14-25 – U.S. First Division suffers a shocking defeat by German armour at the Battle of the Kasserine Pass

Also this month – Wilson appointed C-in-C Middle East

MARCH

2 – German forces begin to withdraw from Tunisia

20-28 - British Army forces punch through the Mareth Line in Tunisia

APRIL

6-7 - American forces from the West link up with British forces from the East in North Africa

MAY

7 – Allied forces capture Tunis

13 – German and Italian forces surrender in Tunisia. The Allies take over 250,000 prisoners

16 – The famous 'Dam Busters' raids see RAF Lancasters strike at German dams

19 - Churchill addresses American Congress

JUNE

20 – Auchinleck becomes C-in-C India

JULY

5 – The Battle of Kursk begins, seeing an epic clash between German and Soviet armour

9-10 – Allied forces invade Sicily (Operation Husky)

25 – Hamburg is struck by Operation Gomorrah – the heaviest air assault in history up until that time

25-26 – Mussolini is arrested and his fascist government falls; Italy enters into talks with Allies

AUGUST

19 – Roosevelt and Churchill meet in Quebec.

SEPTEMBER

3 – British forces land in mainland Italy

8 – Italy officially surrenders

11 – German forces seize Rome

12 – German special forces rescue Mussolini

16 – British forces begin the Dodecanese Campaign in the Aegean

23 – Mussolini re-establishes his fascist government

16TH MAY 1943: Wing Commander Guy Gibson (in door of aircraft) and crew before No. 617 Squadron's raid on the Ruhr Dams

1943: Reconnaissance photo of the Moehne Dam before the raid

AUGUST 1943: Locals aboard a Shermar Mk III tank in the village of Milo, Sicily

OCTOBER

1 – Allies seize Naples, which is already in revolt against its German occupiers

3 - Churchill appoints Lord Louis Mountbatten as the Commander of South East Asia Command.

13 – Italy declares war on Germany

20 – Wavell appointed Viceroy of India

NOVEMBER

28 – Churchill, Stalin and Roosevelt meet at the Tehran Summit

DECEMBER

24 - Eisenhower appointed the Supreme Allied Commander in Europe.

27 - Eisenhower is officially named head of Operation Overlord

1944

JANUARY

6 – Soviet troops enter Poland

17 – First battle of Monte Cassino begins

22 – Allies launch Anzio landings in Italy but become quickly bogged down

27 – The Russian city of Leningrad is finally liberated after 900 days of Nazi siege

Also this month – Wilson appointed as Supreme Allied Commander in the Mediterranean & Brooke promoted to Field Marshal

MAY

11 – The Fourth Battle of Monte Cassino begins

18 – Allies win the Fourth Battle of Monte Cassino

23 – Allied forces launch fresh break-out from the Anzio Beachhead

25 – U.S. General Mark Clark disobeys British General Alexander's plan to trap German 10th Army and instead heads for Rome

JUNE

4 - Allied forces enter Rome

5 – D-Day is postponed for 24 hours due to rough seas

6 – D-Day. 155,000 Allied soldiers assault the beaches of Normandy

13 – First V-1 rocket bomb lands in England

21 – British and Commonwealth forces go on the offensive in Burma

JULY

9 – British and Canadian forces liberate Caen in France

20 – Germany army attempts – but fails – to kill Hitler in a bomb plot

AUGUST

15 – Allies invade Southern France (Operation Dragoon)

19 – Soviets attack Rumania

12TH JUNE 1944: At Montgomery's mobile headquarters in Normandy

6TH JUNE 1944: Canadian soldiers on Juno Beach

25 – Paris is liberated by the Allies

31 – The governing of France is returned to Free French forces

SEPTEMBER

1 – Montgomery is promoted to Field Marshal

3 – Brussels liberated by the British 2nd Army

8 – First V-2 rocket explodes in Britain

17 –20 - Operation Market Garden sees Allied paratroopers dropped on Dutch town of Arnhem on the Rhine. The operation fails

17 – Black out in Britain is replaced with a 'Dim Out'

26 – Soviet forces seize Estonia

OCTOBER

9 – Churchill and Stalin discuss post-war 'spheres of influence' at the Moscow Summit

14 – Allies liberate Athens

14 - Field Marshal Rommel, suspected by the Nazis of being disloyal, commits suicide to prevent retaliation against his family

18 – Hitler orders that all men from 16 to 60 should be called up to defend the Reich

NOVEMBER

2 – Belgium liberated, largely by Canadian forces

4 – Last German forces evacuate mainland Greece

4 – Field Marshal Dill dies

6 – Roosevelt wins his fourth term as U.S. President

DECEMBER

3 – British Home Guard is stood down

4 – Greek Civil War begins between democratic and communist forces

12 - Alexander succeeds Wilson as Commander-in-Chief, Mediterranean

16 – German armour spearheads a massive counterattack against the Allies in the Ardennes Forest

1945

JANUARY

1 – German forces begin to retreat from the Ardennes

12 – Wilson confirmed as Head of British Joint Staff Mission in Washington

17 – Soviet forces seize Warsaw and install puppet government

Also this month - Wilson promoted to Field Marshal

FEBRUARY

4-11 – Churchill, Roosevelt and Stalin meet at Yalta

8 - Paraguay declares war on Germany and Japan

12 - Peru declares war on Germany and Japan

13-14 – The controversial 'firebombing' raids on Dresden take place

CIRCA 1944: Deliver for "D" Day! poster

17TH SEPTEMBER 1944: 1st Paratroop Battalion, 1st (British) Airborne Division, take cover in a shell hole outside Arnhem

1944: Homes destroyed by the Camberwell Road Rocket explosion. V-bomb damage

25 - Turkey declares war on Germany and Japan.

MARCH

4 - Finland declares war on Germany – and backdates it to September 15, 1944

7 – Allies capture a bridge across the Rhine at Remagen.

22-23 – Allied forces cross the Rhine at Oppenheim.

24 – Allied forces under Montgomery cross the Rhine

27 – Last V-2 rocket attack against London

29 – Last V-1 rocket bomb attack against London

31 - Eisenhower broadcasts a demand for the Germans to surrender

APRIL

12 – President Roosevelt dies

12 – Harry Truman becomes President of the United States

18 – All German forces in the Ruhr surrender

21 – Soviet forces reach Berlin

23 – Goering asks to be Hitler's successor. Hitler responds by sacking him and expelling him from the Nazi party

24 - Himmler tries to organise a secret surrender deal, brokered by the Red Cross. It fails – and Hitler orders him to be shot on sight

28 – Mussolini is captured by partisans and executed

28 – Allies seize Venice

30 – Adolf Hitler commits suicide

MAY

1 – Goebbels and his family commit suicide

2 – German forces in Italy surrender

2 – The battle for Berlin ends when German General Helmuth Weidling surrenders to Soviet General Vasily Chuikov

3 - Éamon de Valera, Prime Minister of Ireland, offers his sincere regrets to German officials after hearing of Hitler's death

4 – Montgomery receives the official surrender of German troops in Denmark, Northern Germany and the Netherlands

7 – Germany announces its unconditional surrender to the Allies

8 - Germany announces its unconditional surrender to the Soviets

8 – V.E. (Victory in Europe) Day declared.

9 – German forces surrender on The Channel Islands

11 – The German Army in Czechoslovakia surrenders

23 – Heinrich Himmler, head of the SS, commits suicide

JUNE

5 - The Allies agree to divide Germany into four areas of control.

18 – First demobilisation of the British armed forces begins

JULY

6 - Norway declares war on Japan.

16 - First atomic bomb test

17 – Potsdam Summit sees the Allies demanding the unconditional surrender of Japan. America hints at its new

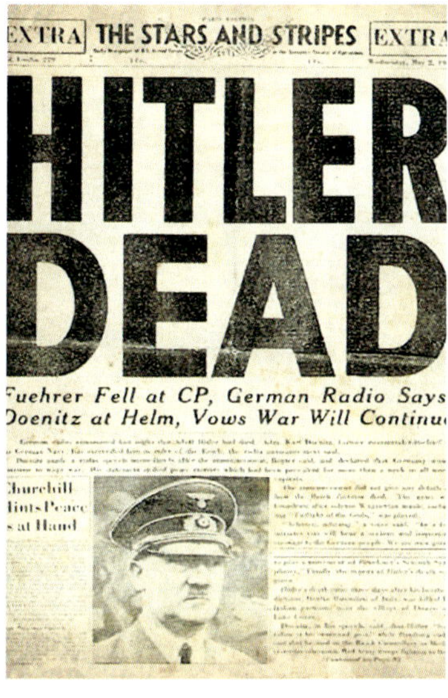

EXTRA THE STARS AND STRIPES EXTRA

HITLER DEAD

Fuehrer Fell at CP, German Radio Says

Doenitz at Helm, Vows War Will Continue

Churchill Hints Peace Is at Hand

2ND MAY 1945: Stars and Stripes announcing Hitler's death

EXTRA THE STARS AND STRIPES EXTRA

VICTORY

Nazis Reveal Surrender To Western Allies, Russia

The unconditional surrender of Germany to the Western Allies and Soviet Russia was announced by the German high command yesterday morning.

The official announcements from the Allied governments are expected to come simultaneously from Washington, London and Moscow today.

The British Ministry of Information, proclaiming that today would be 'Victory in Europe Day,' said Prime Minister Churchill would make 'an official announcement' at 3 PM.

President Truman said he had agreed with the British and Russian governments that no surrender proclamation would be made 'until simultaneous announcements could be made by the three governments.'

King George VI of England sent Gen. Eisenhower a cablegram last night congratulating him and his armies on the 'complete and crushing victory' in Europe.

The Associated Press broke the news of the surrender in a story from Rheims, France, that the Allies had announced Germany's surrender at 0241 hours yesterday morning. It said the surrender took place in the little red school house that is Gen. Eisenhower's headquarters.

Nazis Still Fight Reds At Prague

Prayer, Tears, Laughter —The World Celebrates

8TH MAY 1945: Stars and Stripes announces V.E. Day

8TH MAY 1945: Churchill waves to crowds in Whitehall on the day he broadcast to the nation that the war with Germany had been won

secret weapon – the atom bomb

26 – Churchill loses the general election and is replaced as Prime Minister by Clement Atlee

AUGUST

6 – First atomic bomb dropped on Japan at Hiroshima

8 – The Soviet Union declares war on Japan and invades Manchuria

9 – Second atomic bomb dropped at Nagasaki

14 – Japan agrees to unconditional surrender

15 – V-J (Victory over Japan) Day announced (Truman would later suggest it should be marked on September 2nd)

27 – Remaining Japanese forces in Burma surrender

SEPTEMBER

2 - The Japanese Instrument of Surrender is signed on the deck of the USS Missouri

CLOCKWISE FROM TOP LEFT: FEBRUARY 1945: Yalta summit, Winston Churchill, Franklin Roosevelt and Joseph Stalin sit in foreground; AUGUST 1945: Crew of the Enola Gay, the plane that made the historic flight over Hiroshima to drop the first atomic bomb; The atomic bomb, Little Boy before being loaded into Enola Gay's bomb bay; 9TH AUGUST 1945: Infamous mushroom cloud over Hiroshima **| OPPOSITE PAGE** 14TH AUGUST 1945: Celebrating the surrender of Japan in Times Square NY
NEXT PAGE SPREAD JANUARY 1943: Churchill's delegation at the Casablanca Conference, Morocco

'History shall be kind to me. For I intend to write it.'

Winston Churchill (attrib.)

'I wonder if any historian of the future will ever be able to paint Winston in his true colours. It is a wonderful character, the most marvellous qualities and superhuman genius mixed with an astonishing lack of vision at times, and an impetuosity which, if not guided, must invariably bring him into trouble again and again.'

General Brooke

Churchill's parents, Randolph & Jennie Churchill

WINSTON CHURCHILL

Winston Leonard Spencer Churchill was born on November 30th 1874 into quintessentially Victorian England. Victoria was on the throne, Disraeli was prime minister and the British had just concluded another obscure colonial conflict (The Third Anglo-Ashanti War) after the natives agreed to stop practicing human sacrifice. Three months before, Parliament had voted to end the use of small children as chimney sweeps. It had only been nine years since the end of the Civil War in America and the abolition of slavery. Churchill would be a toddler when the Lakota Sioux, Northern Cheyenne, and Arapaho tribes destroyed the Seventh Cavalry at Custer's Last Stand. He would have just become a teenager as Jack the Ripper stalked the streets of Whitechapel.

When Churchill passed away on January 24th 1965, Harold Wilson was at No10 and the Beatles were at No2 in the UK charts with 'I Feel Fine', (with co-vocals by John Winston Lennon, who had been named for Churchill). The Gemini space programme was just getting underway and U-2 spy planes were streaking over the communist bloc at 70,000 feet. Petula Clark had recently gone 'Downtown' and England was on the very verge of 'swinging'.

In between lies something of a story.

Churchill was born at Blenheim Palace. The rumours say he was actually born in a toilet there. Apparently that's not true although, when asked, Churchill merely said that he couldn't remember. His mother Jennie was an American socialite of no little beauty and his father, Lord Randolph, was an aristocratic Tory politician of no little thrust and ambition who became known variously as 'Cheeky Randy' and 'the Champagne Charlie of Politics.' They were busy people with careers to forge, balls to attend and hunts to ride to and so neglected their son quite horrifically, even by Victorian standards. Jennie was icily remote and Randolph thought the little boy was retarded, barely spoke to him and genuinely disliked him.

From the ages of two to six, Churchill lived in Dublin where his father was in employment to his grandfather, the Viceroy. His mother carried on socialising and his father politicking and the young Winston was left in the care of his nanny, Mrs Elizabeth Everest. The little boy called her *'Old Woom'* or sometimes *'Woomany'* – and came to adore her. That did not prevent him from causing her continuous grief though. If he didn't agree with something, the little Churchill would kick and scream, run off and hide or – on one memorable occasion when faced with a maths lesson – play on Mrs Everest's devout Christianity by falling to his knees and threatening to worship graven images unless he was excused the lesson. The word 'monster' was used quite frequently in the Churchill household. His maternal grandmother called him,' *a naughty, sandy-haired little bulldog'* and young Winston's dancing teacher called him *'the naughtiest boy in the world.'* But still Mrs Everest loved him and the boy responded to her in return.

Blenheim Palace 

CIRCA 1881: Churchill, in Dublin, Ireland

CIRCA 1889: Jennie Churchill with John & Winston

1895: 2nd Lieutenant Winston Churchill of the 4th Queen's Own Hussars

Churchill did not turn on his parents. Instead he loved them. His mother, he said, was like a solitary, beautiful, unreachable star and he worshipped her from afar. His father he held in awe for his power and importance. They did not know this, and probably wouldn't have cared if they did. While his parents had little time for the boy, they did see that he was well provided for with toys. There were tops and magic lanterns and steam trains, but young Winston's favourites were his collection of lead toy soldiers, of which he amassed almost a thousand. Great battles and vast campaigns were fought across the nursery floor. On the rare occasions when his younger brother Jack was allowed to join in, the young Winston would always fix the outcome of the fight, often by ensuring that little Jack didn't receive any artillery pieces in his army. It was now he decided that he wanted to be a soldier – either that, or a politician like his father.

Churchill was educated at St. George's School, Ascot, and Brunswick School in Hove, before ending up at Harrow School in the spring of 1888. He was not a happy boarder. The correspondence that survives between Churchill and his mother consists mostly of pleas for her to visit him or for him to be allowed to come home. The pleas fell on deaf ears. Churchill did not impress at Harrow – at least at first. At the end of his first term, his housemaster reported:

'I do not think ... that he is in any way wilfully troublesome: but his forgetfulness, carelessness, unpunctuality, and irregularity in every way, have really been so serious ... As far as ability goes he ought to be at the top of his form, whereas he is at the bottom.'

He did however become the British Public Schools' fencing champion at the age of 17.

When Churchill finally escaped Harrow School in 1893, he applied for entrance to the Royal Military College, Sandhurst. He failed the entrance exam. Undaunted he tried again – and failed again. It was only on his third attempt that Churchill was accepted. Once inside, Churchill applied for cavalry training - as that required lower marks and a poorer standard of maths than a career in the infantry – and Churchill hated maths. He graduated 8th in his class in December 1894 – after being accused of everything including house theft at Sandhurst - and joined the 4th Queen's Own Hussars as a second Lieutenant the following February.

Ever the flamboyant and high-living aristocrat. Churchill could not possibly afford to live on the £300 salary the Hussars gave him. His mother arranged for him to receive a further £400 a year, but even the two sources of income combined couldn't keep up with Churchill's taste for the high life. To further supplement his income, Churchill decided he would become a war correspondent. He went first to Cuba, where there was a handy little war going on between the Spanish authorities and local

1896: Winston Churchill on horseback, taken while serving with the 4th Queen's Own Hussars in India

CIRCA 1900: 26-year-old Winston Churchill on a lecture tour of the United States

1902: Winston Churchill with Consuelo Vanderbilt at Blenheim

1904: Winston Churchill

rebels to write about for the Daily Graphic. He was shot at for the first time, received his first medal and discovered his lifelong passion for Cuban cigars. Unfortunately at this time his beloved nanny Mrs Everest was dying. He stayed with her in her last week of life and then recorded in his diary:

'She was my favourite friend.'

In the winter of 1896, Churchill was transferred to Bombay with his regiment and soon proved himself an exceptional polo player. Instead of returning to England on leave in 1897, Churchill asked for permission to join the British Army brigades fighting Pashtun rebels on the North West Frontier. He saw heavy fighting in the Mamund Valley and submitted numerous columns for The Pioneer and Telegraph Newspapers. His book on the campaign, 'The Story of the Malakand Field Force', while garnering good reviews upset senior military men as it appeared that a jumped up little junior officer was telling them how to run a proper war. Churchill would go on to write another 42 books during his lifetime.

By now Jennie Churchill was taking some degree of interest in her son. Lord Randolph had died in 1895 aged just 45, the victim of either a brain tumour or syphilis depending on who you believe. (Churchill himself always believed it was syphilis – and Lord Randolph had once told his wife, *'what does an occasional cook or housemaid matter?'* while confessing to his sister-in-law that he fancied rough women – *'the rougher the better'*.) He had achieved the lofty heights of Chancellor of the Exchequer and leader of the House of Commons, but had also made powerful enemies thanks to his personality which seemed to combine principle and sarcasm in almost equal measure. It was a pattern his son was doomed to repeat.

In 1898, Churchill wanted to report on Kitchener's campaign in the Sudan, but found his way blocked by senior officers annoyed by his earlier book. Churchill implored his mother to have a quiet word with His Royal Highness, the Prince of Wales. This was not hard for her to do, as he was one of her estimated 200 lovers. It was not one of history's great love affairs. She called him *'Tum-Tum'* because he was grossly fat and he told her to wear kimonos because they could be easily removed.

Whatever Jennie's real influence, in 1898 Churchill was permitted to join the 21st Lancers in the Sudan. The campaign was the culmination of two years of meticulous planning by the British Army. Kitchener's intent was to smash the forces of the Khalifa Abdullah, the successor to the 'Mad Mahdi' who had killed General Gordon at Khartoum many years before. The Mad Madhi himself was dead and buried, but Abdullah had declared a caliphate and was now threatening to spread his brand of radical Islam to Egypt.

CIRCA 1907: Winston Churchill and White Rhino in Africa

CIRCA 1907: Churchill and friends during their African adventure

After passing some time shelling the Mad Mahdi's tomb for target practice, Kitchener finally enticed Abdullah to come out and fight. Abdullah's army, consisting of some 40,000 Dervishes, was formidable. The British only numbered 8,000 British troops and 17,000 empire troops – but the British forces were professional - and had both artillery and large Maxim machine guns. The 16,000 spearmen and riflemen deployed by Abdullah walked straight into the guns and were simply decimated. Kitchener now swept onwards towards the city of Omdurman and it was here that the 400 men of Churchill's 21st Lancers were used to clear the way. Encountering what they thought was a smallish force of Dervishes they charged, only to discover a further 2,500 men waiting for them in hiding. Incredibly the 21st Lancers prevailed and drove off the Dervishes. Three Victoria Crosses were won in the action and Churchill later wrote that he had killed at least three men. It was the last great charge ever made by British Cavalry.

The Battle of Omdurman was a huge success for the British. 10,000 Dervishes were killed and another 13,000 were wounded in the fighting (and were left to fend for themselves afterwards with no medical treatment.) The British lost 47 men. Abdullah escaped on his donkey – only to be killed a year later at the battle of Umm Diwaykarat. Kitchener personally saw to it that the 'Mad Mahdi's' tomb was demolished and that his bones were dumped in the River Nile. Allegedly, he kept the man's skull and had it turned into a drinking vessel.

Churchill resigned from the British Army in 1899 to follow in his father's footsteps and pursue a career in politics. He stood for the Conservatives at Oldham – and very quickly lost to his surprise. A bit perplexed as to what to do with himself now, Churchill secured a paid job with the Morning Post as a war correspondent and sailed off to South Africa, where the Second Boer War had just broken out. While there, he joined a British armoured train on a scouting mission, got caught up in a fierce skirmish and ended up as a Boer prisoner of war. He promptly escaped with a £25 dead or alive bounty on his head, travelled almost 300 miles to safety and then wrote a letter taunting the Boer Commander.

Churchill's exploits made him something of a legend back in Britain - and indeed internationally as the tale of his daring escape had been followed by newspapers around the globe. There was talk of him being awarded the Victoria Cross and music hall singers of the time sung about him in popular ballads. Instead of returning home to enjoy his celebrity however, Churchill stayed on in South Africa, joined the South African Light Horse and entered into both Ladysmith and Pretoria.

Upon his return, he stood again for the Conservatives in Oldham at the 1900 general election. This time he was a bona fide celebrity and so this time he won. To capitalise further on his fame, Churchill then set off on a speaking tour around Britain, followed by tours of America and Canada. Mark Twain himself introduced

CIRCA 1907: Churchill on a cow-catcher in Africa

1907: Churchill and King Daudi of Uganda watching a war-dance at Kampala

the young Churchill to New York. For this, Churchill received almost the equivalent of a million pounds in payment.

Churchill's parliamentary career saw him get into trouble with his own party almost straight away. He rebelled against the orthodoxy of the Conservatives and voted against them on both military expenditure and protectionist tariffs. His own constituency party disowned him and Churchill eventually crossed the floor to join the Liberals. Distinctly unwelcome in his Oldham constituency, Churchill instead stood as a Liberal in the seat of Manchester North West in the 1906 general election. After two years, due to the complexity of parliamentary laws, he lost the by-election there and re-emerged as an MP for Dundee. Now a member of the Asquith cabinet, Churchill distinguished himself by establishing the first minimum wages seen in Britain, by setting up the nation's labour exchanges and by helping to draft Britain's first unemployment pension legislation. However, he also showed a dubious interest in the growing novelty that was eugenics and campaigned for the sterilisation of the 'feeble minded'. He was unsuccessful.

On September 12th 1908, Churchill married Clementine Hozier. Many of their friends gave the couple six months at best. Despite some rough patches – Clementine once threw a plate of spinach at Churchill in her exasperation with him – they were together for fifty-six years. They were to have five children together – Diana, Randolph, Sara, Marigold and Mary between 1909 and 1922.

When appointed Home Secretary, Churchill found himself in more trouble. He was falsely accused of sending troops against striking miners in the Rhondda Valley. In fact, he held them back. In January 1911, he personally directed operations at Sydney Street in London, where criminal Latvian anarchists were under siege and wanted for the murder of three police officers. Barracked by the crowd with shouts of *'who let them immigrants in then?'* Churchill shocked everyone by calling up a contingent of Scots Guards from the Tower of London and setting them on the anarchists. During the ensuing fight the house caught fire – and Churchill personally stopped the fire brigade from putting it out. The anarchists died in the flames. He later commented:

'I thought it better to let the house burn down rather than spend good British lives in rescuing those ferocious rascals.'

Churchill also found himself in a no-win situation over the growing issue of women's suffrage. His compromise solution was to suggest holding a referendum to let the nation decide but he was overruled by Asquith on the matter.

In 1911, Churchill became First Lord of the Admiralty and was still with the Admiralty when the First World War broke out. One of his first actions – sending the 1st and 2nd Naval Brigades to the besieged Belgium port of Antwerp - helped gain time for Dunkirk and Calais to be secured. He was also – by a strange quirk of fate

1909: With German Emperor Wilhelm II during a military manoeuvre near Würzburg, Bavaria

CIRCA 1907: The "Terrible Twins" David Lloyd George and Winston Churchill

1912: Winston Churchill, then the British Colonial Secretary, in Ottoman Damascus

– instrumental in developing the very first tanks, when the British Army showed no interest in the project and left it for the Navy to explore.

However, Churchill was also one of the planners of the disastrous Gallipoli campaign of 1915 and its terrible outcome was both to haunt him and inform his strategies long into the next war. The Great War was barely four months old when Churchill suggested starting a 'second front' in the Dardanelles, attacking Germany's ally Turkey with an assault on the Gallipoli Peninsula. By doing this, he said, the Russians could be supported, Turkey could be knocked out of the war and Germany subjected to far more pressure. The Turks, Churchill believed, were the enemy's weak link. Thanks to some confusion at a top level war council meeting, Churchill thought he had got permission to proceed with the plans he had been drawing up. He hadn't – and it was only the first of many mistakes.

By mid-February 1915, British warships were shelling Turkish troops and fortifications in the Dardanelles, while 70,000 British and Dominion troops prepared to embark from Egypt. The Navy's effect on the Turkish ground forces proved stubbornly ineffective. On March 18th 1915, disaster hit the British fleet. Three battleships were sunk by mines and another three badly damaged and knocked out of action. With the Royal Navy limping back to Alexandria to refit, the Army decided it was time to take over.

As the Allied troop ships steamed for Gallipoli, no one really knew who was in charge of things, and no one realised that they had not got the necessary authority to launch the attack. However, the Allied Commanders were of a single mind. Turkish troops were simply no good and would crumple when faced with cold steel. In actuality, the forthcoming Allied invasion had been such a poorly kept secret that the Turks had had time to build powerful new defensive positions and increase their troop numbers in Gallipoli six fold.

Allied troops started going ashore on April 25th. Three of their beach landings were unopposed. A fourth saw Turkish resistance which was overcome. However, the landing at Sedd-el-Bahr was a slaughter. Turkish machine gun posts swept the water. Many troops failed even to make the beach and there were vivid reports of a sea full of bodies. The ANZAC landings saw fighting so ferocious that officers on the beach asked for permission to abandon the assault. They were refused.

By May, the casualty rate on the Allied forces was appalling. Medical facilities were overwhelmed and many troops were falling sick in the unsanitary conditions and blistering heat. They were still largely confined to the immediate area around their landing beaches and pinned down. In August, tens of thousands of extra Allied troops were thrown against Sulva Bay in conditions of such secrecy that no one had any idea what they were

1912: Churchill inspecting the boys from a training ship 

INFLEXIBLE
NAVY ESTIMATES
TORY
F. H. TOWNSEND 1914

supposed to be doing. The attack failed to link up with the ANZAC forces pinned down at Anzac Cove and the Allies were beaten back again.

Churchill had lost his position as First Lord of the Admiralty by now, as the Liberal government had fallen and been replaced by a coalition. He was still allowed a place on the War Council though. By December, everyone could see that the Gallipoli campaign was both a shambles and a disaster. The surviving Allied troops were withdrawn in a series of staged evacuations between December 1915 and January 1916.The Allies had suffered over 200, 000 casualties, as much from disease as from enemy action.

Churchill would be forever scarred by Gallipoli. During the Second World War, the horrors of a sea full of British bodies at Sedd-el-Bahr made him extremely hesitant to launch an Allied invasion of Europe and he would fight hard against the eager Americans to prevent it from happening for as long as possible. The humiliating losses also made the older Churchill just a little fixated on the Mediterranean theatre and inspired him to make strategic moves that were not always for the best. It was also at this stage of his life that Churchill took up painting as therapy. He would continue to paint almost up until his death – and produce almost 600 canvases.

Bitter at being side-lined and, frankly, bored, Churchill resigned from the government and went to fight. Awarded a temporary rank of Lieutenant Colonel on January 5th 1916, he became Commander of 6th Battalion, the Royal Scots Fusiliers, and fought on the Western Front. Three months later, he was home again, having made 36 daring forays into no-man's-land on individual missions.

In July 1917, Churchill was reintroduced to politics by his good friend David Lloyd George and appointed Minister of Munitions. When peace broke out he went on to serve as Secretary of State for War and Secretary of State for Air. Now he provided fierce support for intervention in the Russian Civil War – and much to the disgust of the Labour Party, was instrumental in arming the Polish forces invading the Ukraine. Churchill also unleashed the infamous Black and Tans in the Irish War of Independence.

In 1921, the Churchill's three-year-old daughter Marigold contracted septicaemia while on holiday at the seaside and died. It was a shattering moment for the family. The following year, still stumbling to come to terms with their loss, the Churchills purchased a new home. Chartwell, near Westerham in Kent, was close to being a ruin when they found it, but Churchill set about doing it up. It was both a home and therapy. He built – amongst other things - a swimming pool, a fish pond and large red brick walls to enclose the vegetable garden and in the process became such an accomplished bricklayer that he joined the Amalgamated Union of Bricklayers. He was later thrown out for being a Tory. Nevertheless, he would continue to indulge his odd – and oddly therapeutic – love of bricklaying for many decades. His other hobbies developed at Chartwell included cultivating roses and butterflies, while he also took every opportunity to return to painting. Churchill would need to find new forms of therapy throughout his life. He suffered chronically from depressive illness, which he referred to as his 'Black Dog' and it could be nearly crippling when it overtook him. His hobbies and activities provided some escape, but often not nearly enough. Sometimes, he felt close to suicide, confiding:

'I don't like standing near the edge of a platform when an express train is passing through. I like to stand right back and if possible get a pillar between me and the train. I don't like to stand by the side of a ship and look down into the water. A second's action would end everything.'

Chartwell was soon full of odd, tatty and bizarre animals. Churchill had always been a true animal lover - at age 17 he had sold his beloved bicycle to purchase Dodo, his beloved bulldog. He found their company very therapeutic and Chartwell became home to quite a menagerie over the decades with everything from black swans on the lake to pigs – Churchill's favourite animals. He kept a succession of parrots, parakeets, goats, budgies, cats and dogs. Chickens would wander around inside the house, encouraged on by the younger Churchills. Later in the 1940s, Churchill added a working farm to the Chartwell estate but it failed to make any money as he refused to let the animals be slaughtered. He said that you couldn't possibly kill an animal after you had wished it good morning. Exotic pets over the years included a kangaroo and a duck-billed platypus. He was given a lion called Rota and a leopard called Sheba but both had to be donated to London

14TH JANUARY 1914. Satirical cartoon from Punch magazine, depicting his Conservative Party colleagues approval to his proposals for funding the navy

9TH OCTOBER 1918: The Minister of Munitions Churchill meets female workers at Georgetown's filling works near Glasgow

19TH JULY 1919: Churchill chatting to General John Pershing at the Victory Parade in London

Zoo. At home, the Churchills even gave each other animal names. Churchill was 'Pug', Clemmie was 'Kat,', Randolph was 'Rabbit', Diana was 'Puppy Kitten' and Mary was 'Mouse'.

This intensely kind and humane side of Churchill is both instructive and serves as a useful comparison. While at a wartime conference, Churchill once confided in Josef Stalin that he was rather fond of goldfish. The Soviet Dictator then assured him that he could arrange for Churchill to have a plateful for breakfast.

In the 1922 general election, Churchill lost his seat in Dundee after falling ill from all the stress while campaigning. He stood again as a Liberal candidate in Leicester in 1923 – but lost. He would finally return as a 'Constitutionalist' candidate, after winning the seat at Epping. The notion of a new Constitutionalist party soon fell out of fashion and Churchill accepted the post of Chancellor of the Exchequer in Stanley Baldwin's Unionist government. *'Anyone can rat, but it takes a certain ingenuity to re-rat,'* Churchill commented as he re-joined the Conservative Party.

Churchill was by no stretch of the imagination a successful Chancellor. That's hardly surprising, since he was lousy with money in his own personal life. The annual bill from his wine merchant was – at one time – more than three times what a manual working man earned in a year. He would struggle to control his spending all his life. As Chancellor, he returned Britain to the Gold Standard – a move he later described as the greatest mistake of his life. Deflation hit the British economy. Unemployment soared. Manufacturing costs exploded. The miners went on strike and this in turn led to the General Strike of 1926.

It was at this time that Churchill – briefly – had an odd flirtation with fascism. While it's almost certainly not true that he was prepared to use machine guns on striking miners, he let everyone know where he stood by declaring *'either the country will break the General Strike, or the General Strike will break the country.'* He praised Mussolini's fascist Italy as showing the way to stand up against communism and said that il Duce had *'rendered a service to the whole world.'* Churchill even called Mussolini a *'Roman genius ... the greatest lawgiver among men.'*

Churchill's political standing seemed to be at an all-time low – but worse was to come. In 1929, the Conservatives lost the general election and Churchill began to lose interest in his political party. He became more hostile to their ideas and took friends from the media and from finance rather than from the political classes. He also lost a lot of money of his own in the Wall Street Crash. Churchill's 'Wilderness Years' had begun, relegated to the back benches with no party leader willing to give him a cabinet post.

28TH MARCH 1921: Mr. and Mrs. Winston Churchill at Government House reception in Jerusalem, Palestine

1921: Churchill and Herbert Samuel

Now Churchill devoted more time to his writing, producing a biography of his illustrious ancestor John Churchill, 1st Duke of Marlborough and working on his epic 'History of the English Speaking Peoples'. He wrote prolifically on politics too. Amongst his stranger ideas was a plea to abandon universal suffrage. He had seen what increasing working class influence had done to nations in the 1920s and thought it too dangerous to allow, as it could permit socialist or even communist rule in Britain. *'The best argument against democracy is a five-minute conversation with the average voter,'* he concluded.

Churchill was also at this time a leading voice against the idea of Indian independence. He simply hated Gandhi, whom he thought a charlatan – a well-educated, westernised lawyer playing dress up in a loincloth. He said

'It is alarming and also nauseating to see Mr Gandhi, a seditious Middle Temple lawyer, now posing as a fakir of a type well known in the East, striding half-naked up the steps of the Vice-Regal Palace ... to parley on equal terms with the representative of the King-Emperor.'

If Ghandi wanted to go on hunger strike, let him die, Churchill believed. *'The truth is,'* he said, *'that Gandhi-ism and everything it stands for will have to be grappled with and crushed.'* He even went so far as suggesting that Ghandi ought literally be crushed:

'(He) ought to be lain bound hand and foot at the gates of Delhi, and then trampled on by an enormous elephant with the new Viceroy seated on its back.'

Churchill loved the notion of Empire, but this was not his sole reason for arguing against Indian independence. He believed that it would have savage economic effects on British industry and elsewhere, but his main concern was that India itself would be riven and perhaps even destroyed by internal civil war once freed. With no little foresight, he anticipated the horrors of Partition which were to come.

The future of India was, however, not Churchill's main concern. That was Nazi Germany. He could see that Germany was on the rise again and, by 1932, considered himself the sole warning voice. No one wanted to face what an ascendant and rapidly rearming Germany would really mean or the prospect of another war as terrible as the Great War.

Britain, like many nations, had been all too quick to beat most of their swords into ploughshares after 1918 to enjoy the benefits of a 'Peace Dividend'. Now, they had far too small an army to fight even a continental war, let alone protect the far reaches of empire. Influential voices in the Dominions were also telling Britain that, should war break out in Europe again, this time they could not be relied upon to provide troops.

Many people in Britain – of all classes – did not see Hitler as a natural enemy. Some believed Germany had been treated too cruelly in defeat in 1918 and that Hitler's actions and demands were really quite reasonable. He would, they said, simply stop after he had achieved a measure of justice. Moreover, with its roots in strong ties between state and business, the rise of fascism seemed like a solution to growing communism in Europe. Even Churchill admitted as late as 1937 that – forced to make a choice – he would choose fascism over communism.

Churchill was trying to get his concerns about the rise of the Nazis heard on the BBC, but finding himself blocked. The BBC was then the tool of the establishment, and the establishment did not want the British public to hear what Churchill – with his famously potent oratory powers – wanted to tell them. Furthermore, the founder of the BBC, Lord Reith hated Churchill. He was *'essentially rotten...a swine...(and) unfit to govern'* he would later write. Churchill hated him back, saying *'I absolutely hate him.'* While Reith might not have had time for Churchill, he did have rather a soft spot for Hitler, writing in his diary that the Nazis *'would clean things up.'* Churchill was permitted to give a radio talk on the dangers of German rearmament once - in 1934 – and was then never again allowed to speak on the subject on the BBC until the start of the Second World War.

In February 1936, Nazi Germany invaded the Rhineland. It was essentially a test of French and British resolve, and German troops had orders to withdraw if the French intervened militarily. They didn't. It caused chaos in the British Parliament. The national government were divided between wanting to apply economic sanctions and being terrified of their failure. The Labour opposition wanted no sanctions against the Nazis at all.

Appeasement had become the official policy. Churchill was utterly horrified when his old friend Lloyd-George met with Hitler in 1936 and returned to Britain claiming the Fuhrer was *' a man of supreme quality.'* Churchill called appeasement *'a defeat without a war'* and defined an appeaser as *'... one who feeds a crocodile - hoping it will eat him last.'* While appeasement was undeniably widely popular in Britain with everyone from pacifist Labour MPs to Conservative communist-haters to the ordinary people of the nation who didn't want war, appeasement didn't work. It only emboldened the fascists. They saw it as weakness, pure and simple, and pressed ahead secure in the knowledge that they would not encounter the only opposition they respected – direct military force.

In 1937, Germany and Italy openly fought alongside the fascists in the Spanish Civil War. The rest of Europe did nothing as German bombers devastated the town of Guernica and other Spanish targets. On March 12th 1938, the German 8th Army crossed into Austria and declared it was now Ostmark, a province of Germany. Prime Minister Chamberlain merely held up his hands and said that nothing could have been done to stop them unless Britain was prepared to use military force. Hitler noted that no one had opposed him and was further emboldened.

In September 1938, Chamberlain essentially tried to force Czechoslovakia to give Germany all the territory it was demanding – known as the Sudetenland- without firing a shot. He told the Czechs they would have to stand alone if they resisted. Churchill was almost a solitary voice in warning:

'The partition of Czechoslovakia under pressure from England and France amounts to the complete surrender of the Western Democracies to the Nazi threat of force. Such a collapse will bring peace or security neither to England nor to France.'

Chamberlain was later to sniff that the whole affair was *'a quarrel in a faraway country, between people of whom we know nothing'.*

At a meeting in Munich to which the Czechs were not invited, Chamberlain gave Germany the go ahead. Germany took the land they wanted and Chamberlain returned to Britain with a piece of paper which he waved before the newsreel camera crews assembled at Heston Aerodrome and claimed that he had secured 'peace for our time'. As a reward, Chamberlain was invited to stand alongside the King and Queen on the balcony of Buckingham Palace to receive the cheers of a grateful nation. After the Munich agreement, Churchill said in the house:

'You were given the choice between war and dishonour. You chose dishonour, and you will have war.'

But things went on and the world was not much bothered. Time Magazine declared Adolf Hitler to be their 'Man of the Year'. And

OCTOBER 1939: Churchill finds time to read a book at his home in Chartwell, Kent

28TH AUGUST 1940: Winston Churchill viewing activity in the Channel from an observation post at Dover Castle during his tour of defences

23TH OCTOBER 1940: Churchill and General Władysław Sikorski, Prime Minister of the Polish Government-in-Exile inspecting troops of the 1st Polish Rifles Brigade at Tentsmuir

then - on March 16th 1939 - Hitler simply invaded the rest of Czechoslovakia and then turned to look at Poland. A day later, an exasperated Chamberlain told the world that Hitler could no longer be trusted not to invade other nations. On March 31st, he guaranteed to defend Poland should it be attacked. It's very probable Hitler didn't believe him.

On September 1st 1939, 62 German divisions crossed the border into Poland, supported by 1,300 fighter and bomber aircraft. That same day, Poland requested military assistance from Britain and France. Deadlines were drawn up for a German withdrawal Hitler refused to blink and Britain finally declared war on September 3rd 1939. Winston Churchill was now a part of the War Cabinet under Chamberlain and also re-appointed as First Lord of the Admiralty. The Royal Navy were delighted, and a message went out to the fleet saying simply:

'Winston is back'.

And then not much happened. Poland was quickly torn to pieces between the invading Germans and Russians and everything went quiet for months on end. The anticipated bombing raids didn't come, there were no apocalyptic gas attacks and when hostilities happened they almost always broke out at sea. *'It's better to be bored than bombed',* Chamberlain said philosophically. Churchill disagreed.

Churchill, being Churchill, was never able to confine himself to just matters pertaining to the Royal Navy. Every day it seemed like he had a new – and very urgent - idea for Prime Minister Chamberlain to consider: The RAF should start bombing Germany; Britain should seize Norway for its iron ore deposits; the state of the French Army needed better understanding; Cabinet and other government jobs should be swapped around; the Royal Navy should move into the Baltic in force. His unheeded suggestions filled the 'Phoney War' that raged – or rather did not rage – for a good eight months. Churchill was the sole voice calling for action, while his colleagues were more than content to let things continue as they were. Then it all blew up in their faces.

The 'Phoney War' came to an abrupt end when Germany invaded Norway and Denmark at the start of April 1940. As chairman of the Ministerial Coordination Committee, Churchill plunged into a new frenzy of activity, trying to bully the military men about him to stir them into action. Every day he had new ideas. Every day they were different. Major General Ismay had to work desperately hard behind the scenes to stroke ruffled feathers among the brass and to prevent, as the civil servant John Colville put it *'a first class row'.* In the end, Churchill got so excited and things got so fraught that Chamberlain had to take control of the committee himself. It was an excellent indicator of what was to come.

17TH JULY 1940: Churchill helps to build a pillbox at Canford Cliffs, Poole, England, during a visit to Southern Command

On May 10th 1940, with the Germans now in control of Norway against lacklustre British opposition, Chamberlain resigned as Prime Minister. It was obvious that Parliament no longer had faith in him to run the war effort and his attempts to form a unity government were firmly rebuffed by the Labour Party. Churchill was appointed Chamberlain's successor at a meeting between Lord Halifax, Chamberlain, Churchill and the government's chief whip David Margesson. He was sixty-five years old.

The decision to appoint Churchill as Prime Minister was a compromise and one not particularly welcomed by many in the Conservative Party or the House of Lords, who met the announcement of Churchill's appointment as PM with cold silence. Even his introduction to the House of Commons was greeted with a 'lukewarm' reaction, while the outgoing Chamberlain received rapturous applause. A large proportion of the establishment, still not completely dissuaded of the virtues of fascism, were looking to see the war concluded by a negotiated settlement and not by an aggressive, eccentric renegade with no sense of the political realities of the day.

Hitler was equally unimpressed when he heard Churchill was now Prime Minister. He regarded him as nothing more than a drunken incompetent and a 'puppet of Jewry'. Churchill smoked too much, lived too extravagantly and was undisciplined. Hitler much preferred the cut of Soviet Dictator Josef Stalin's jib, which should probably not come as any surprise.

Churchill became Prime Minister on the very day Nazi Germany unleashed its Blitzkrieg against the Low Countries and additionally created the post of Minister of Defence, which he also took for himself. The war would be fought - and fought his way. One of his first acts was also to create a coalition government, and to establish a War Cabinet consisting of himself, Neville Chamberlain, the Foreign Secretary Lord Halifax, Clement Attlee and Labour's deputy leader Arthur Greenwood. The War Cabinet met nine times in late May, with Lord Halifax pressing for a negotiated peace settlement with the Nazis to be brokered by Italy. He'd even gone so far as to tentatively broach the subject with the Italian Ambassador on his own initiative. Churchill wasn't interested. *'My policy,'* he declared, *'is a policy of war.'* He wanted to fight – and win. *'Those (nations) which surrendered tamely were finished,'* he believed. On May 28th,he told the extended

19TH MAY 1940: Churchill leaves 10 Downing Street with Irish journalist and Minister for Information Brendan Bracken cabinet, *'If this long island story of ours is to end at last, let it end only when each one of us lies choking in his own blood upon the ground'*. This shut Lord Halifax up good and proper.

Churchill attacked his new task with such energy and single-mindedness that his wife Clementine actually became alarmed at his behaviour. She wrote to him, saying,

'My darling, I hope you will forgive me if I tell you something I feel you ought to know. One of the men in your entourage, a devoted friend, has told me there is a danger of your being generally disliked by your colleagues and subordinates because of your rough, sarcastic and overbearing manner. My darling Winston, I must confess I have noticed deterioration in your manner and you are not so kind as you used to be.'

There were good reasons why. In private, Churchill wasn't at all sure that Britain could win. By May 16th, it was becoming increasingly obvious that the French Army was no match for the German Wehrmacht – and indeed neither were the ten British divisions at war in Europe. They and their Commanders were geared to small police actions in the colonies, not massive continental campaigns utilising the latest in panzer and warplane technology and tactics. By the 16th, Churchill was in France to see for himself just what was going on. While he conferred with the French warlords at the Quai d'Orsay, junior officers raced back and forth across the lawns, desperately burning secret documents. British forces had already been outflanked and, back in England the next day, Churchill was already thinking of evacuation and the impact of the inevitable fall of Paris. Even as the British troops were being rescued off the beaches of Dunkirk in late May, the Director of Military Intelligence actually told a BBC correspondent, *'we're finished.'* On 12th June 1940, in a particularly low mood, Churchill confided to General Ismay, *'You and I will be dead in three months' time'*. He had already drafted the speech he would make on the radio when the invasion arrived. It would end: *'The time has come – kill the Hun!'*

Churchill's private fears were most certainly not to be reflected in his announcements to the nation. On May 13th, he had made his first speech as Prime Minister to Parliament:

'I would say to the House as I said to those who have joined this government: I have nothing to offer but blood, toil, tears and sweat.'

On June 4th, with the emergency evacuation of the British Expeditionary Force from Dunkirk and the prospect of a German invasion to fall upon the nation in short order, Churchill had told the nation:

'We shall go on to the end. We shall fight in France, we shall fight on the seas and oceans, we shall fight with growing confidence and growing strength in the air, we shall defend our island, whatever the cost may be. We shall fight on the beaches, we shall fight on the landing grounds, we shall fight in the fields and in the streets, we shall fight in the hills; we shall never surrender.'

After making the speech, Churchill confided to a friend, *'And we'll fight them with the butt ends of broken beer bottles because that's bloody well all we've got.'*

On June 18th, with the prospect of an aerial blitz by the German Luftwaffe followed by a sea full of invasion barges increasingly likely, Churchill gave his 'Finest Hours' speech to the House of Commons, saying:

'...the Battle of Britain is about to begin. Upon this battle depends the survival of Christian civilisation ... Let us therefore brace ourselves to our duties, and so bear ourselves, that if the British Empire and its Commonwealth last for a thousand years, men will still say, This was their finest hour.'

It was the third of three quite exceptional speeches designed to rally not just Parliament but the entire nation – and to make Churchill's defiance of Hitler clear in an international arena. The three speeches combined galvanised a hesitant Parliament and steeled a nation. Those words were, in the words of one Labour MP, *'worth 1,000 guns and the speeches of 1,000 years'*. When someone asked Clement Attlee after the conflict precisely what Churchill did to win the war, Attlee replied acidly: *'Talk about it.'* One further crucial speech was to follow.

On August 16th 1940, at the height of the Battle of Britain, Churchill made a personal visit to No. 11 Group RAF Operations Room at

CIRCA 1940: Churchill inspecting the damage inflicted by incendiaries to the Debating Chamber of the House of Commons ▶

8TH SEPTEMBER 1940: Churchill visits bombed out buildings in the East End of London

Uxbridge. Returning to his staff car, he silenced General Ismay saying that he had never been so moved in his life as by what he had just witnessed. After a few moments, he murmured *"Never in the field of human conflict has so much been owed by so many to so few'.* The words stayed with him, and formed the heart of his famous speech on August 20th.

The Battle of Britain was essentially a defensive battle for Britain, as would be the response to the invasion should it come. This was not at all how Churchill wanted to fight a war. From his earliest days as Prime Minister he had been looking for ways to take the fight to Hitler. The phrase 'Action this day' dominated if not his thoughts then at least his dreams. Just two days after the final troops had been pulled off the beaches of Dunkirk, he was asking for reports to be drawn up on the best ways to land tanks on a beach. He began to establish offensive units such as paratroopers and commandos. On July 10th 1940, in a letter to Lord Beaverbrook, he fantasised about an *'absolutely devastating, exterminating attack by very heavy bombers from this country upon the Nazi homeland'* and set about creating a potent bomber force. By late summer he was considering re-invading Norway. On July 22nd, he established the Special Operations Executive, designed to send agents into occupied Europe and help set up resistance movements. The purpose of the SOE was, he said *'to set Europe ablaze'*

The accidental bombing of London by a sole Luftwaffe aircraft which had lost its way gave Churchill a chance to finally take the war to the enemy as he had dreamed, sooner than he had thought. On August 25th 1940, 95 RAF bombers struck 'in retaliation' against Berlin. They did little damage to the city – but the raid had enormous psychological effects on the Nazi leadership. Goering had promised that *'no enemy bomber would ever fly over the Reich'.* He was proved a liar. Hitler was almost insanely furious that another nation should have the gall to do this to his people. Until now, German bomber attacks on Britain had been directed against airfields and air defences. Now the Fuhrer ordered the bombing to be switched to Britain's cities instead. The RAF had gained a valuable respite – and Hitler's decision may well have changed the outcome of the whole Battle of Britain – but the Blitz had begun.

As London shuddered and strained under air raids, Churchill

1940: Firing an automatic gun at an armament factory being watched by spectators made a point to go out almost every single morning to meet the people of London, often joined by the King and Queen. They were cheered through the streets. At night, if he could evade those charged with his protection, he would sneak up on a rooftop and watch the Blitz unfold. At weekends he practiced rifle and pistol shooting for the hour when the invasion came. Observers said he was both serious about it and conducted his shooting with a degree of relish.

Since he became Prime Minister back in May, Churchill had been officially fighting the war from the Cabinet War Rooms which were acting as the nerve centre of the war effort. The idea of a central 'War Room' had been dreamed up in December 1937 to house the civilian War Cabinet and top military Commanders. It was suggested that it could be in located one of three places – in central London, to provide immediate shelter in case of bombing in the first days of war, out in the London suburbs where it was still convenient for the organs of power but away from the epicentre of bombing, or completely away from any major town or city deep in the heart of the West Country.

The London location chosen was a converted basement below the New Public Offices at the corner of Great George Street and Storey's Gate. This was only meant ever to be a stop gap location, until something purpose built and altogether safer and more suitable could be constructed. The rooms were just ten feet underground and no one was sure how they might stand up to a direct hit from a bomb.

The War Rooms were officially opened on August 27th 1939 and were already in use by the time war was declared on September 3rd. Plans to move out of the temporary base continued but at a snail's pace. It just didn't seem urgent. No one was bombing London, so the War Cabinet continued to meet in Downing Street. The Chiefs of Staff continued to use what were now called the Cabinet War Rooms, as did the JPC – the Joint Planning committee – and the number of support staff grew around them. When Churchill visited the underground cabinet room in May 1940 he said, *'This is the room from which I'll direct the war'*. He didn't want to. It felt cowardly to him to duck down away from the action, and he didn't fancy, to use his own term, becoming a 'trog', but he recognised the value of a central command area where he could personally lead – and dominate. All of his top Commanders could be within easy reach, instead of being stationed all over London where they could scheme or plot or duck him. He had them in his sight and in his grasp.

Down in the War Rooms, relations between Churchill as his Commanders became difficult almost immediately – and stayed that way for the rest of the war. Churchill behaved just the same way he had when he had chaired the Ministerial Coordination Committee back during the Norwegian Crisis. He considered himself an expert on military matters and wasn't afraid to tell the Generals their business. He pouted. He shouted. He interfered. He sneered. He even cried. Churchill thought that the war could only be won by dash and daring. Looking at his Generals, he found them somewhat lacking in the dashing and daring stakes. They were cautious, even timid sometimes.

Although he thought of himself as a military man, Churchill was first and foremost a politician – and he treated his Commanders now as rival politicians. Politics was vicious, cold and rude and altogether a rougher game than the generals were used to. They were, to a man, quite hurt by such brusque behaviour. Gentlemen did not treat gentlemen this way. It was left to Churchill's chief staff officer General Ismay and to his Chief of the Imperial General Staff or CIGS (General Dill and then Brooke) to smooth things out and translate the PM's gruff abuse into more diplomatic language. When he arrived in 10 Downing Street, the CIGS was General Ironside. Churchill had already fallen out with him quite mightily over the invasion of Norway and he was gone the same month. Following him was General Dill. He lasted almost 19 months under Churchill's withering demands before he was given the boot. *'Old Dill-Dally'* Churchill called him, scornful of his lack of dash. Only when General Brooke was appointed at the very end of 1942 did Churchill finally meet his match. Brooke was made of tougher stuff than Dill, and could stand up to Churchill even if it secretly brought him close to cracking up in private.

While the top men played politics and waged war, around them all buzzed a mix of military and civilian staff, male and female, often young, servicing the needs of the various departments. The War Rooms expanded but still became more and more crowded. Those working there took to calling the place 'the bunker' or 'the hole'. It smelled of cigarette, pipe and cigar smoke. It smelled of numerous colognes and perfumes, some luxurious, some cheap.

1941: Winston Churchill aboard HMS Duke of York, saluting his youngest daughter Mary, an N.C.O. in the A.T.S.

CIRCA 1941: With General KM Loch, Frederick Lindemann, and others at anti aircraft drill

9TH JANUARY 1941: Churchill raises his hat in salute during an inspection of the 1st American Squadron of the Home Guard at Horse Guards Parade in London

It smelled of over-used chemical lavatories. The staff forced to live in the sub-basement had to contend with rats, cloying damp, the ceaseless and irritating hum of the ventilation system and the lights being kept on 24 hours a day. The young attractive women working as secretaries or telephonists found themselves the centre of sometimes unwanted attention from every male in the bunker from the Royal Marines guarding the entrances to the top brass. *'There goes a fine filly!'* General Ismay was heard to exclaim rather enthusiastically upon more than one occasion. But it was wartime.

Churchill lived in the modified number 10 annexe with his wife just above the War Rooms from December 1940 onwards. There, he established a highly defined routine for himself. He was woken up at eight thirty and then had breakfast before spending virtually the rest of the morning in his four poster bed, reading newspapers and attending to the documents brought in to him. General Ismay could usually be found by his bedside taking orders. Reading done, Churchill then took a bath and went for a large and lavish lunch in defiance of all rationing. Lunch would be served at 1.30 pm precisely. Then he'd have a nap and another bath, head off for dinner and then attend evening meetings and catch up on other work with his secretaries. They could be expected to work to his whim until about 4.30 in the morning. Officers might be summoned and expected to work into the wee hours as well. General Ismay once begged Churchill to let him sleep, Churchill told him petulantly, *'well, if you don't care who wins the war, you go ahead'.*

A further shock to those who worked closely with Churchill was his cavalier attitude to semi and full nudity. He seemed quite unperturbed for his officers or staff to see him wrapped in his red, green and gold dressing gown or – on too many occasions –, just wrapped in a large fluffy bath towel. General Brooke memorably described him as *' looking rather like Humpty Dumpty with...small thin legs'.* Sometimes he would just parade around wearing only his personally-tailored pale pink silk underpants. If he felt like it, he might dictate a letter or memo from his bathtub to some poor unfortunate young secretary whose only defence would be to avert her eyes and think of England.

Weekends were often spent at Chequers with important house guests – Generals, Ambassadors and Ministers. Churchill did not stop working, but did allot time for games of croquet or tennis and for rambling walks in the Chiltern Hills. The guests ate lavishly and each night watched a film – all too often 'That Hamilton Woman' starring Vivien Leigh, which was one of Churchill's favourites and which made him cry. Then he would hold court on matters both philosophical and practical until the early hours while his house guests just wanted to go to sleep. Winston needed very little sleep – and couldn't seem to ever understand that he was almost

21ST NOVEMBER 1941: Outside 10 Downing Street

CIRCA 1941: Distinguished company at the Headquarters of the Canadian Corps, General Wladyslaw Sikorski , Lieutenant- General AGL McNaughton , General Charles de Gaulle

unique in this. He would finally wave them off to bed with the familiar words, 'Goodnight, my children.'

Arthur Harris, Commander in Chief, RAF Bomber Command was a frequent houseguest at Chequers and recalled:

'I think the first thing that impresses one about Winston is the extraordinary mixture in him of real human kindness and of sometimes impish mischief, all overlaid with an immense, thrusting, purposeful determination to reach the goal which he so clearly sees. The affection which the whole Churchill family feel for one another is very obvious and most refreshing.'

General Auchinleck, dining there in 1941, recalled,

'Winston was most affable and terribly interesting...He is a very attractive personality and really amazing for his age. He never seems to tire. I do not know how he does it...When I went off Winston was still listening to martial music on the gramophone!'

'KBO,' mumbled Churchill frequently. It stood for *'Keep Buggering On'*. And KBO he did. With the threat of German invasion reduced by the end of 1940, Churchill found himself at a bit of a loss as to what to do next. The Army didn't seem to be being put to much use. Indeed, there was a sour joke going around with the Blitz still on that the Army were being used to knit socks for the civilians in the trenches. Attlee later said, *'(Churchill) was always looking around for 'finest hours' and if one was not immediately available, his impulse was to manufacture one.'* CIGS Dill understood this and was worried about it, desperately hoping that Churchill would not insist on a disastrous campaign just for the need for another 'finest hour'. Churchill's attention had now focused pretty much on North Africa and the Middle East – the one theatre where Britain had significant armed forces and where it could act aggressively. Here Churchill ferociously and relentlessly pressed his Commanders in the field to launch offensives. Inaction drove him mad with frustration. *'The Admirals, Generals and Air Marshals chant their stately hymn of 'safety first...How bloody!'* he complained in a bitter letter to his son Randolph.

And indeed General Dill did think the best strategy was to wait it out, avoid defeat ... and wait for the Americans to save the day. Churchill for his part feared that if he didn't achieve some major successes soon, the Americans would lose faith in him and he would lose all the goodwill the Battle of Britain had generated in America. Then, they wouldn't come at all.

And then, in June 1941, Hitler made the greatest strategic blunder of the war. He invaded Soviet Russia. Operation Barbarossa saw the Third Reich throw almost four million German soldiers, 3,580 panzers, 7,184 artillery guns and 1,830 aircraft from the Luftwaffe

26TH MAY 1942: Delegates enjoying a walk in the gardens of 10 Downing Street, following the signing of the Anglo-Soviet Alliance

20 NOVEMBER 1942: Churchill inspects the new Lee-Enfield No. 4 Mk 1 rifle during a visit to 53rd Division in Kent

against Russia. The Soviet Union was now in the war and Churchill at last had a fighting ally, albeit one he neither liked nor trusted. Churchill's attitude to Stalin was pragmatic. He bit his lip, sucked on his cigar, did what he had to do and said what he had to say. After Operation Barbarossa, Churchill famously said, *'If Hitler invaded Hell, I would at least make a favourable reference to the Devil in the House of Commons.'* All of his attitudes towards 'Uncle Joe' need to be understood in that light. After Barbarossa, Churchill immediately started promising – and delivering – war supplies to the beleaguered Russians, even though he feared that, by the following year, Moscow would most probably be a 'gone coon.' Stalin was both boldly ungrateful and haughtily unimpressed. What he wanted was a second front, for Britain to invade France and to take the pressure off his own armies. He would keep calling for it, monotonously and aggressively, until D-Day.

Stalin was a little man in a big job. Just 5 foot 4 inches in his socks (Truman called him *'a little squirt'*), and with a deformed left arm and terrible smallpox scarring all over his face, Stalin had to work extra hard to maintain his strong image. Any artist painting his portrait either greatly flattered him or else took a bullet. His real name was Losif Vissarionovich Dzhugashvili. He chose the name Stalin because it roughly meant 'man of steel'. His most notable contribution to the First World War had been to get a 13-year-old girl pregnant, he'd spent the later part of the 1920s encouraging top scientists to breed a human-ape super-hybrid and he was already a tyrant and mass murderer on a scale perhaps greater than Hitler. He was not the friend Churchill wanted, but he had lots of soldiers and he was killing Germans.

The friend Churchill wanted beside him was of course the United States but now it was almost two years into the war and there was still no sign of them. Back in May 1940 with the Germans rampaging through France and the invasion looming , Churchill had confided in his son Randolph: *'I think I see my way through .... I mean we can beat them!' Randolph asked him how. Churchill beamed and replied. 'I shall drag the United States in.'*

But the United States weren't having any dragging, even though President Roosevelt himself was broadly sympathetic to the British cause. Roosevelt might have been a natural ally, but that was not necessarily true of his nation. America had strong isolationist leanings. It did not want to get involved in another colossal war of Europe's making. One Gallup poll in 1940 showed that Americans opposed getting involved by a ratio of 13 to 1. The nation also had a sizable population of German descent who favoured Hitler, a very large Irish Catholic community who instinctively opposed any British campaign, a misguided radical left that saw Hitler as a very good man because he was then friends with Stalin ('FDR please/ FDR please/ Don't you send me overseas' sang Woodie Guthrie) and a growing fascist movement of its own that held

1942: Churchill standing in a doorway his hand raised in a victory gesture

rallies inspired by Nuremberg and children's camps inspired by the Hitler Youth. Also America's Ambassador to Britain in 1940 was one Joe Kennedy, a Catholic of Irish descent who had written Britain off already and was constantly trying to stop his President from getting involved in a war the country had already lost.

In 1940, America had been more than happy to sell Britain things – but at absolutely full price. America bled Britain – and smiled while it did so. America wanted Britain to keep fighting but it also wanted it economically damaged. It already had its eye on a post-war world where the British Empire was gone and its colonies were free to trade with America. People in Britain talked about our American 'friends' in inverted commas. There were even suggestions that every British couple should melt down their gold wedding rings to help pay the crippling debt that trade with America was racking up. In 1940, Britain did succeed in negotiating 50 destroyers from America in exchange for base rights in British territories, but they were old and clapped out and by the end of 1940, only nine were still at sea. In 1941, Arthur *'Bomber'* Harris sneered, *'up to date they have had a damn fine war. On British dollars. Every last one of them'.* Harris also suggested that the Americans had only escaped their Great Depression by leaching off of British money during the early war years. Lease-Lend when it came eased the burden, but there was still much bitterness.

When Churchill first heard of the devastating Japanese surprise attack on the US naval base at Pearl Harbor in December 1941, his thoughts were entirely selfish. He was delighted. He knew then, he said:

'We had won the war. England would live; Britain would live; the Commonwealth of Nations and the Empire would live ... Hitler's fate was sealed. Mussolini's fate was sealed. As for the Japanese, they would be ground to powder. All the rest was merely the proper application of overwhelming force.'

On December 11th, Germany and Italy formally declared war on America.

Within just a few days of Pearl Harbor, Churchill was on his way to America to discuss waging war together. This wasn't an entirely new concept to the American High Command. Under the top

◀ 1942: Inspecting the Home Guard

JANUARY 1943: Accompanied by Air Chief Marshal Sir Charles Portal, leaving Consolidated Liberator "Commando" of No. 24 Squadron RAF at Lyneham, Wiltshire

CIRCA 1943: Shaking hands with Wing Commander M T Judd, leader of No. 143 (Canadian) Wing,

secret 'Plan Dog' auspices, the High Command had been modelling and wargaming such an eventuality since October 1940. Churchill sailed to America aboard the battleship Duke of York, accompanied by General Dill whom he had only just fired as CIGS. It was December in the Atlantic. The journey was rough and those in Churchill's party who suffered from sea sickness found their misery amplified by the clouds of thick cigar smoke emanating from the Prime Minister. Churchill himself was almost unique in not getting sick. The crossing took twice as long as usual and the battleship didn't arrive in America until December 22nd. Churchill however thrived on the journey. His doctor, who accompanied him, said that the Prime Minister was a changed man.

'A younger man has taken his place ... a month ago, if you had broken in on his work, he would have bitten off your head. Now at night, he is gay and voluble, sometimes even playful.'

After docking, Churchill and his party then flew down to Washington where Roosevelt himself met them at the airport. Churchill stayed as a guest in the White House. The first Anglo-American war summit was code-named Arcadia and it was a triumph for Churchill.

America had been geared up for war with Japan in the Pacific, rather than war with a European foe in the Atlantic. It had consequently greatly enlarged its fleet at the expense of its army and – to an extent – its air force. It had been Japan, not Germany, that had attacked America so treacherously at Pearl Harbor, sinking eight battleships and killing over 2,000 people. Other American interests in the Pacific were under dire threat. Americans were baying for Japanese blood. And yet Churchill and his team still managed to persuade their American counterparts on the policy of 'Germany First'.

Another huge success was Churchill's speech to the American Congress, given on Boxing Day 1941. He talked of partnership – and parentage, reminding the congressmen that he was indeed half-American himself – and it was a triumph. The standing ovation was deafening and seemed to go on forever. The American Secretary of the Interior, Harold Ickes said that Churchill was *'the greatest orator in the world'.* He then had lunch with Congress, returned to the White House and promptly had his first heart attack. It was kept very secret.

Churchill eventually returned to Britain on board a Boeing Clipper, arriving home on January 17th 1942. Although Roosevelt liked him, he had found Churchill very demanding emotionally, and exhausting company. He was also not particularly taken by Churchill's habit of wandering around the White House naked of a night, or of the Prime Minister's comedy double act with Lord Beaverbrook, comprising corny jokes and impersonations.

FEBRUARY 1943: Churchill with General Montgomery and other senior officers of the Eighth Army, Tripoli

MAY 1943: With Admiral of the Fleet Sir Dudley Pound on the SS Queen Mary

1ST JUNE 1943: Churchill salutes allied troops in the amphitheatre at Carthage, during a visit to troops near Tunis

Churchill, for his part, thought he had achieved everything he needed – but he hadn't. The Americans had their blood up. They wanted to get at Hitler straight away. They wanted to invade Europe right now in 1942 and get things settled. Churchill and his new CIGS General Brooke were horrified. They had really severe doubts about the state and the calibre of the American Army. They saw that American war planning was naïve and clumsy– and they had very private doubts about the quality of the American Commanders, most of whom had never been in combat. Hitler was too strong, his fighting forces too good and any invasion launched now would almost certainly fail. What's more, the invasion of Europe in 1942 would have involved largely British forces as America's army was still too small and untrained to take a serious role. Of course, there was no proper way to communicate this to their new ally.

It is again to the credit of Churchill and Brooke that they would be able to divert the Americans from this course of action and turn them instead to war in North Africa and the Mediterranean – a theatre the Americans would normally have no interest in. By fighting here, the British reasoned they could weaken the Germans and wear them down. At the same time, the RAF and the U.S. Army Air Force (USAAF), would pound Nazi Germany relentlessly from the air – the Americans by day and the RAF by night. While the Germans grew weaker and their manufacturing capacity was progressively reduced, America would have time to build and train a better army and get its mighty industrial base churning out an unstoppable torrent of guns, ships, planes and tanks.

Once again, Churchill would get his way – but at a price. It soon became increasingly clear that America was not interested in being a junior partner in the venture. Or a silent one. Churchill progressively found it harder and harder to get his own way. Where once in the darkest months and years of the war he had stood alone, the sole power, now he was himself increasingly the most insignificant member of a triangle comprised of himself, Roosevelt and Stalin.

At home, there were challenges in Parliament. Old party rivalries started to resurface and there were whispers that Churchill might be forced to stand down, perhaps in favour of Stafford Cripps. The public, galvanised by Churchill in the summer of 1940, were now tired of bad news and of war – and far less ready to fight. The unity of the 'thems' and 'us's' was fracturing. Strikes flared up amongst vital war workers and British communists were baying for an early invasion of Europe to help Uncle Joe. The war was going badly – perhaps due to Churchill's poor grasp of strategy. Everyone was blaming everyone else. The Generals were dull and incompetent. British conscripts lacked the fighting spirit. British tanks were poorly designed and small arms inferior to the German issue. Britain was fighting a foe superior in every way except morally – and what did that count for?

1944: LEFT TO RIGHT: Lord Athlone, Franklin D Roosevelt, Winston Churchill and Mackenzie King in Quebec, Canada during the Ottawa conference

26TH AUGUST 1944: Discussing the battle situation in Italy with Lieutenant General Sir Oliver Leese (left) and General Sir Harold Alexander, Monte Maggio area

7TH AUGUST 1944: Churchill and General Montgomery & his dog, Rommel in Normandy

By the end of 1942 Churchill was finding it all too much. Everything was too big and complicated. Jewish leaders were making him aware of the Holocaust, which he was powerless to stop. There was Operation Torch, the fall of Tobruk, massive setbacks in the Far East including the loss of Malay and Singapore, no real progress on the Eastern Front, the Siege of Malta, U-Boats running amok in the Atlantic, the Dieppe Raid ending in failure, vast diplomatic complexities, American public opinion turning against the British. – and the latest reports said that RAF night bomber offenses were next to useless. They couldn't hit precise targets. Churchill agreed to them flying against the one target big enough for them to hit – cities. It wasn't how he wanted to wage war. On one occasion, he was observed to sit and cry for ten minutes solid.

Now the Black Dog savaged him with increasingly regularity and ever-greater cruelty. He realised that, after the war was over, America and the Soviet Union would come to divide up the spoils and that they would not hesitate to take chunks of the British Empire as part of those spoils. He would be helpless to stop these competing military leviathans once they got going. Friends would be enemies and nothing would be as it was before.

The Casablanca summit in January 1943 was very pleasant. Witnesses record Field Marshals and Admirals rushing down to the beach to make sandcastles after a hard day's negotiating. Behind the scenes though, tensions however between the Americans and the British were very real. America did indeed want more control of the direction of the war. In private, the British and Americans bad-mouthed each other. The American top brass were angry and jealous that Churchill seemed able to exert more influence over their president than they could. Admiral King – an American who really disliked the British – kept wanting to direct shipping straight off the slipway and into the Pacific theatre. General Marshall was again angling to invade France with Operation Roundup and to go straight for the Nazi jugular with 30 divisions. D-Day must come in 1943, he insisted. Brooke's answer was to turn Marshall and King against each other. How could a European invasion be launched in 1943 when all the shipping and landing craft were being sent to the Pacific? At the closing of the summit, Roosevelt announced that he would accept nothing short of 'unconditional surrender' from Germany. This worried Churchill, as he thought that might be considerably harder to achieve from a proud nation still so bitter from the terms of Versailles. Churchill came back from the conference with more doubts. In Russia, Stalin – who hadn't attended the summit for fear of being deposed in his absence - was driven to rage when no firm date was set for a second front:

'Hundreds of thousands of Soviet people are giving their lives in the struggle against fascism, and Churchill is haggling with us

12TH JUNE 1944: Churchill lights a cigar in the back of a jeep while touring the Normandy beaches with General Mongomery

11TH NOVEMBER 1944: General Charles De Gaulle and Winston Churchill leaving the Arc de Triomphe. Paris

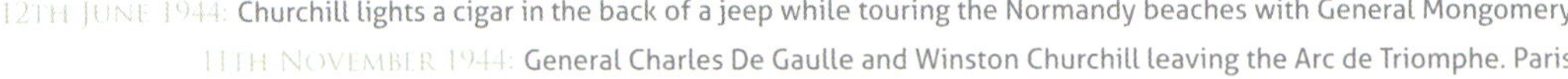

T69

15TH JULY 1945: Stepping off his airplane at Gatow, Berlin, Germany, en route to the Potsdam Conference

16TH JULY 1945: Accompanied by his daughter, Mary, during the Potsdam Conference

27TH JUNE 1945: Making a speech in Uxbridge, Middlesex, during the general election campaign

about two dozen Hurricanes. And anyway those Hurricanes are crap ...'

By mid-1943, the Americans were deeply suspicious of the British. They thought the British were afraid of a cross-channel invasion and that Churchill might be – in his dotage – just messing around in the Mediterranean trying to refight the disastrous Dardanelles Campaign of 1915. What's more, the Americans now believed that the British could never be trusted with overall command for D-Day. An American would have to shoulder that responsibility. In late August 1943, Churchill insisted on launching the ill-fated Dodecanese Campaign, despite American refusal to participate. It was Britain's last significant campaign of the war, it failed horribly and after the dust had settled, there was little doubt as to who now really held the power in the Allied partnership.

Travelling to a meeting with Roosevelt in Cairo on board the battlecruiser Renown in November 1943, Churchill was taken ill and the ship put in at Malta. Churchill spent two miserable days convalescing in bed in the residence of the island's Governor, Lord Gort. He spent the two days pitifully begging Brooke to bring him little luxuries off the warship and shouting at the passing Maltese beneath his bedroom window to shut up and go away. When the party finally got to Cairo, Harold Macmillan thought that Churchill looked as if he was seriously ailing. *'One forgets, of course, that he is really an old man,'* he commented, *'But a wonderful old man he is too.'* From Cairo, where Anglo-American tensions over everything from the Aegean and Italy to Operation Overlord and Burma were at an all-time high, the leaders moved on to Tehran to meet with Stalin. This was the first time that Roosevelt had met Stalin face to face, and the President suspected he might have more war aims in common with the tyrant than with Churchill. The two even shared a joke about mass murdering German officers after the war which caused Churchill to storm out. (Stalin for his part had his fellow leader's rooms bugged and every morning would receive fresh transcripts from his secret police of what they were saying in private.) The balance of power was shifting. Both wanted an invasion of France. Churchill was being edged out. He started to see a side of Roosevelt he didn't like, one that allowed him to easily accommodate tyrants rather than the leaders of free nations. He wrote:

'There I sat with the great Russian bear on one side of me, with paws outstretched, and on the other side the great American buffalo, and between the two sat the poor little English donkey who was the only one...who knew the right way home.'

On leaving the conference, Churchill became ill again and eventually ended up diagnosed with pneumonia. Just before Christmas 1943, he had two more heart attacks. He spent

1945: Montgomery welcoming Winston Churchill at Berlin-Gatow airfield

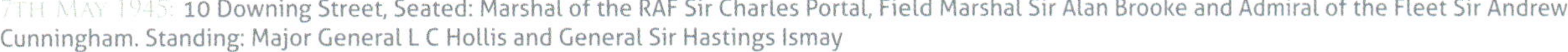

7TH MAY 1945: 10 Downing Street, Seated: Marshal of the RAF Sir Charles Portal, Field Marshal Sir Alan Brooke and Admiral of the Fleet Sir Andrew Cunningham. Standing: Major General L C Hollis and General Sir Hastings Ismay

NAL CORPS

260250

Christmas and the New Year recuperating in North Africa before returning home to England. He surprised everyone by sneaking back into Parliament unannounced and received a huge round of applause, whereupon he burst into tears. Rumours of his illness gripped Britain but – when a courtier at Buckingham Palace showed him to a lift rather than a flight of stairs - Churchill made a point of running up the stairs two at a time and then looking back down and thumbing his nose at those watching him.

Nevertheless, Churchill shrank further back and away. Those who had witnessed the Dodecanese debacle spoke of *'bodies floating in the water'* and Churchill's mind made painful comparisons with Gallipoli. At Chequers on weekends away, he spoke of dying soon – and then inflicted a wealth of Gilbert and Sullivan records upon his guests until the early hours.

Even in early 1944, he was still expressing serious doubts about Overlord and suggested instead a new invasion of Norway, an invasion of Sumatra or another large scale Dieppe style commando raid on occupied France. In secret, he was probably deeply, deeply afraid. It didn't matter now what he wanted. Russia and America had decided. Overlord was on for 1944 and he couldn't stop it anymore. It's possible that Churchill would have slipped further back and away were it not for the fact that General Eisenhower, slated to be in overall charge of the invasion of Occupied Europe, both liked and admired the man and fought to be friendly with him and to keep him in the loop, even when he didn't have to. Eisenhower later wrote of Churchill:

'(He was) an inspirational leader, he seemed to typify Britain's courage and perseverance in adversity and its conservatism in success..... He used humour and pathos with equal facility, and drew on everything from the Greek classics to Donald Duck for quotation, cliché, and forceful slang to support his position. I admired and liked him. He knew this perfectly well and never hesitated to use that knowledge in his effort to swing me to his own line of thought in any argument.... He was a great war leader and he is a great man.'

Churchill had not been wrong in his thinking. The Mediterranean Campaign had helped tie up valuable German resources. In July 1943 there were 18 German divisions spread between the Balkans and Italy. By Christmas 1943 there were 49. The bombing had reduced German war production and Stalin had taken vast chunks out of the Germans on the eastern front, turning the tide at Stalingrad and Kursk.

Churchill's thoughts kept going to the Soviet Union. Looking forward, he saw terrible danger. He warned the Americans of *'bloody consequences in the future...Stalin is an unnatural man. There will be grave troubles.'* In May 1944, he wrote to Eden; *'The Russians are drunk with victory, and there is no length they may not go.'*

Then Churchill found his enthusiasm for the invasion at last. He took his private train down to Portsmouth on the eve of D-Day to visit the troops and made – in Brooke's words - *' a thorough pest of himself.'*

D-Day was a great success. On the night before the landings, Churchill had told his wife that he feared 20,000 soldiers would be killed on the beaches. In reality, the death toll was actually 3,000. The wait the British had insisted on had paid off. Churchill got to visit the invasion beach head on June 12th, but more and more events were out of his control. Everything was very fast and very military now, rather than political.

'I am an old and weary man. I feel exhausted,' he told Macmillan at Chequers one weekend. On August 14th, Brooke recorded in his diary that he thought 'it would be a godsend if he (Churchill) could disappear out of public life ... I have found him almost impossible to work with of late, and I am filled with apprehension as to where he may lead us next.'

Churchill and Roosevelt continued to fight about the Italian Campaign - always a sideshow to the Americans – but Churchill was now keenly aware that he had less influence than ever before. Roosevelt refused to attend a war summit in Britain. He thought it would look bad to be 'summoned' by a lesser ally in an election year. Churchill drank more, fought more and sulked more. New information about the Holocaust reached him that both depressed and enraged him. He wrote:

'There is no doubt that this is probably the greatest and most horrible crime ever committed in the whole history of the world...It is clear that all concerned in this crime who may fall into our

15th July 1945: Inspecting the honor guard at Gatow Airport in Berlin, Germany where he has just arrived to attend the Potsdam Conference

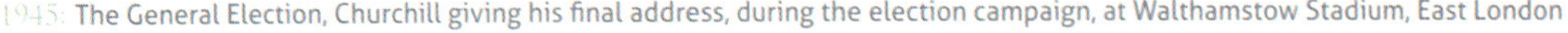
1945: The General Election, Churchill giving his final address, during the election campaign, at Walthamstow Stadium, East London

hands, including the people who only obeyed orders by carrying out the butcheries, should be put to death.'

Even so, he still had no idea of the true scale of the horror. Intelligence officers spoke in terms of thousands being murdered. No one guessed the truth lay in the millions. It was unthinkable. Germany was after all a civilised European nation. They could not possibly be that evil.

By mid-August 1944, Churchill was in the Mediterranean again, interesting himself in the situation in the Balkans, Greece and Italy. As the Germans abandoned Athens, Churchill had men sent in to secure it from communist guerrillas and had General Alexander personally drive him to the frontline in combat gear to see the action and to feel a part of it. He returned to Britain with a serious illness, only to set off again for a fruitless summit scant days later looking, as Brooke recorded *'old, unwell and depressed'*. In October he had a bilateral meeting with Stalin in Moscow, which was again fruitless. After he left, Stalin said with glee, *'We fucked this England!'*

At home and abroad, hostility to Churchill was growing. H.G Wells insisted that *'Churchill must go,'* calling him quite vilely *,'the present would-be British Fuhrer.'* With victory in sight, the international Left was starting to jockey for power in the post-war world. Suddenly, having outlived his usefulness Churchill was no longer a war leader. He was just another Tory.

The Yalta Summit in February 1945 only emphasised Russia's power in the world. A sickening – indeed dying – Roosevelt seemed powerless to resist Stalin, but instead again favoured his communism over Churchill's perceived imperialism. Roosevelt died of a massive stroke on April 12th 1945, weeks from victory. Churchill considered flying out to his funeral but changed his mind. It was a measure of how much his respect for the President had fallen.

In the final weeks of the war, Churchill visited the front lines twice, enormously enjoying being – if not in the thick of the action then in a front row seat. Brooke, who had to accompany him merely rolled his eyes, bit his lip and then wrote in his diary that it was a real relief to get Churchill home again as he suspected the PM would have been rather pleased to have died in battle.

Germany fell, Hitler committed suicide and the war was won. On May 8th 1945 – designated Victory in Europe Day – Churchill went on the radio to announce the surrender of Germany. A full European ceasefire would come into effect at a minute past midnight. Later he spoke before a large crowd gathered in Whitehall, telling them, *'This is your victory!'* The crowd shouted back, *'no, it's yours!'* and sang *'For He's A Jolly Good Fellow'* before Churchill led them in a vigorous singalong to 'Land of Hope and Glory'.

In private, Churchill was not nearly so sure that the war was really over in Europe. The Soviet Union looked very menacing. In fact, Churchill had had secret plans drawn up to launch a surprise attack on the Red Army starting on July 1st 1945. The plan even involved fighting alongside re-armed German Army units against the Soviets. It was called Operation Unthinkable. His Chiefs of Staff Committee obviously agreed with the name – and successfully talked Churchill out of starting World War Three. The Japanese finally surrendered in August 15th 1945, pummelled into shocked submission by the atomic strikes on Hiroshima and Nagasaki – but Churchill was by then no longer in charge.

In July 1945 there was a general election in Britain. Everyone expected Churchill to win. Having just won a world war, what was a general election? Only two months before the election, Churchill enjoyed an approval rating of 83%. Everyone predicted a rousing Conservative victory and the return of Churchill to power. Instead he lost – and no one has ever been quite able to explain why. Why would a nation suddenly sweep their saviour, their great war hero from power? It seemed more than ingratitude: It looked like betrayal.

Churchill's loss in 1945 wasn't just by a narrow margin. It was a crushing defeat by any measure. The Labour Party under Clement Attlee swept into power by a landslide. Churchill was said to be *'both surprised and stunned'*. So why did it happen? Some commentators believe that a war-weary people simply wanted a change. They saw Churchill as a wartime leader and not one for peacetime. Others remembered that it had been the Conservatives who were foremost in appeasing the Nazis in the 1930s and so had brought war down on them. These people liked Churchill, but hated his party. Still others believe that Churchill was too complacent, offering next to nothing new while the

Labour Party offered the earth. Churchill had also upset many on the Left by saying that the Labour Party would force socialism on the nation by use of something akin to the Gestapo. One critic even suggested that Churchill's habit of smoking fat Havanas in front of troops who hadn't been able to scrounge up a half-decent cigarette in days had made him enemies in the ranks! Whatever the truth, whatever the reason, Churchill was out of power.

For six years, Churchill fought on as the Leader of the Opposition. He travelled and lectured around the world, famously giving a speech at Westminster College in Fulton, Missouri in March 1946 where he stated:

'From Stettin in the Baltic to Trieste in the Adriatic, an Iron Curtain has descended across the continent.'

He spoke vigorously in favour of the Commonwealth and the 'Anglosphere' – the English speaking nations – and against the European Coal and Steel Community, the forerunner of the European Union. Wherever Britain's destiny lay he said, it was not in Europe.

Churchill's cousin, Clare Sheridan, provided a fascinating portrait of the Churchill of the time after she had dinner with him in June 1948:

'Winston, in his dreadful boiler suit was looking pale. He rants, of course, about the inefficient ignorant crowd now in power, who are what he calls throwing the British Empire away. He is almost heartbroken... He quoted Hamlet several times which illustrates his spirit of despondency ... '

Churchill was also relatively poor at this time, still writing frantically at all hours to keep the money coming in. Indeed, he was at one point almost bankrupt and on the verge of having to sell Chartwell. Only with help from his friends did he manage to keep it. During this time, he published a massive six part history of the Second World War which was well received by everyone except his wartime Generals. Back in the 1920s, when Churchill had first published his history of the Great War, Balfour had smirked, *'Churchill has written an enormous book about himself and called it 'The World Crisis''*. Now, as far as men like Brooke were concerned, Churchill had once again written an enormous book about himself and this time called it The Second World War. They felt Churchill had exaggerated his own part in the victory and consequently downplayed the role of the military high command. Wartime diaries were liberated from cupboards and lofts in no short order, and even in censored form soon challenged Churchill's own account of events. Brooke's diaries in particular shook everyone with their frank views of Churchill.

In 1951, Churchill led his party back to victory in a general election. He was seventy-seven years old. He built more homes (something Attlee had neglected), lowered taxes, improved worker safety and did whatever he could to keep what was left of the British Empire together. *'I will not preside over dismemberment,'* he said. At the same time, Churchill vigorously promoted the 'Special Relationship' between Britain and America, making four trips to meet with President Eisenhower, even if he didn't always see eye to eye with him. 1953 also saw him win the Nobel Prize for Literature.

Although still blessed with a spritely mind, Churchill's physical health was now beginning to finally fail him. He had suffered his first stroke in the summer of 1949, but it was only mild. Still, while as PM from 1951 onwards, he would often be forced to conduct matters of state from his sick bed. *'I am ready to meet my Maker,'* Churchill had said on his seventy-fifth birthday. *'Whether my Maker is prepared for the great ordeal of meeting me is another matter'*. He was struck by a more severe stroke which affected both his speech and mobility in June 1953, the same year he received his knighthood. He was 78 years old. He returned to political life in October that year, but it was increasingly obvious that he was too ill to continue to exercise the duties of his office.

Churchill resigned from office in 1955 and became a back bencher. He would finally stand down as an MP at the 1964 general election. His daughter Diana had committed suicide the previous year. It was the final blow.

In his last years, Churchill alternated between his London home and his estate at Chartwell, taking long holidays to the French Riviera where he was the toast of high society. He painted to try and keep off his lifelong problem with depressive illness, but

30TH JANUARY 1965: Winston Churchill's coffin on board the barge Havengore at Tower Pier after the state funeral at St Paul's

the Black Dog was coming in for the kill now. It could smell the weakness. Churchill told his cousin Clare Sheridan that he felt like a complete failure and that he was heartbroken that *'the empire I believed in has gone.'* President Kennedy made him an Honorary Citizen of the United States but Churchill was too sick to attend his own ceremony.

On January 15th 1965, Winston Churchill suffered a severe stroke. As he lay dying, there was one solitary photograph by his bedside – that of his nanny 'Woomany', now 70 years dead. Winston Leonard Spencer Churchill died nine days later on Sunday January 24th . He was ninety years old.

They honoured Churchill with the largest state funeral the world had ever known. Even the Queen would attend – against all protocol. The great and the good came to honour him from no less than 112 different nations. Only Communist China sent no-one. After his body spent three days lying in state, Churchill's funeral was held on January 30th 1965. 25 million Britons watched on their TV sets as it was broadcast live all over Europe.

As Churchill's funeral barge passed up the Thames, the dockers of London lowered the jibs of their cranes in a spontaneous salute. The Royal Artillery fired a nineteen gun salute and sixteen English Electric Lightnings from the RAF roared overhead. From Waterloo station, where his coffin was loaded aboard a train pulled by a Battle of Britain class steam locomotive named in his honour, he was taken to Hanborough, close to Oxford and buried by his own request at St Martin's Church, Bladon, near Blenheim Palace.

AND THEN HE WAS GONE.

◀ 30TH JANUARY 1965: The funeral cortege arrives with his coffin at St Paul's Cathedral during his state funeral

'I had, and retain, a great liking and an enormous admiration and respect for (Brooke). I consider he is the best soldier that any nation had produced for very many years.'

General Montgomery

'It is only since I have read (Brooke's) diaries that I appreciate what a consummate actor he must have been. Behind the confident mask was the sensitive nature of a man who hated war.'

General Brian Horrocks

General Alan Brooke sits for portrait on opposite page

BROOKE – THE OTHER HALF

General Alan Brooke was once having an increasingly angry and difficult telephone conversation with Churchill, who was tucked up in bed. Such fraught phone conversations were typical. Then all at once Churchill bellowed down the receiver, 'Get off you fool!' Brooke put the telephone down. He fumed for hours. He seethed. He probably even considered resignation. Only the next day did he discover that Churchill had been shouting at his pet fluffy grey Persian cat, Smoky, who had taken it upon himself to jump on Winston's wiggling toes and then chew on them during the conversation. Brooke would not have been amused when he finally found out the truth. He and Churchill inhabited a very strange world, and enjoyed – if that's the right word – a very strange relationship.

Alan Francis Brooke was born into a distinguished Ulster military family in Bagnères-de-Bigorre, France on July 23rd 1883. His father was Sir Victor Brooke, 3rd Baronet of Colebrooke and Brooke was the youngest of seven children. Sir Victor died when his son was just eight years old while hunting ibex across the Egyptian desert and Brooke became dedicated to his mother, whom he often referred to as *'My dear little pet.'* He was a solitary, self-absorbed and quiet child. He spent his first sixteen years growing up and being privately educated in France before attending the Royal Military Academy in Woolwich, South London. Those who knew the young Brooke at the Academy described him as private, shy and even delicate. 'He is restless and lives on his nerves,' one contemporary wrote about him. Those who would later work with him during the Second World War would recognise the description. After graduating 17th in his year, Brooke was commissioned into the Royal Regiment of Artillery as a second Lieutenant at Christmas 1902 and joined the elite Royal Horse Artillery in 1906. He served in both Ireland and India and particularly enjoyed his posting to the Raj. His brother officers liked him and thought him clever and witty, and he had plenty of time to go big game hunting and to indulge in horse racing. While travelling by train, he rejoiced in sitting next to an open window with a catapult and shooting at the bottoms of natives bent over in the fields.

Immediately prior to the outbreak of the First World War, Brooke married Jane Richardson, a neighbour in County Fermanagh in Ulster. They had been engaged – secretly – for six years, but unable to marry because of money problems. He was almost immediately recalled from his honeymoon to re-join his regiment as Britain mobilised. The couple would have two children, Rosemary and Thomas, before Jane was killed in a car accident in 1925. Brooke blamed himself and would be haunted by guilt for much of his life. He said,

'I very much wish I could have been finished off myself at the same time.'

In 1929, Brooke married for a second time, this time to Benita Lees. The couple would have two children , Kathleen and Victor. Benita

1940

CIRCA 1942: Brooke looking at a globe at his desk in the War Office in London

CIRCA 1942: General Sir Alan Brooke at his desk in the War Office in London

Brooke with Churchill and General Sir Oliver Leese, General Sir Harold Alexander and Montgomery

too would die in a car crash, in 1968.

Brooke served with the Royal Artillery during the First World War and during the Somme Offensive of 1916 made a name for himself by adopting the 'creeping barrage' technique pioneered by the French at Verdun earlier that year. Using the 'Creeping Barrage', infantry could advance with the support of artillery shells landing progressively further away from their lines as they moved forward towards enemy positions. Brooke also planned the artillery barrages in support of the Canadian Corps as they assaulted the German positions on Vimy Ridge in 1917. 1918 saw him appointed as the senior artillery Commander in the First Army at the rank of Lieutenant Colonel, while his outstanding war service had earned him two D.S.O.s.

After the Great War, Brooke now became a distinguished lecturer at both the Staff College, Camberley and the Imperial Defence College, where he would meet – and assess - many of the officers who would later become the senior British Generals of the Second World War. From the mid-1930s onward, he progressed through a number of prestigious roles with the British Army.

With the outbreak of the Second World War, Brooke took command of II Corps, part of the British Expeditionary Force in Europe and waited for the seemingly inevitable attack by the Nazis with some trepidation. He was particularly sceptical of the state of the French Army and thought that they could never hold back the Germans when they came. Brooke's Commander, Lord Gort, who was in charge of the BEF, was aware of Brooke's views and seriously considered replacing him in the field because of what he perceived to be Brooke's defeatist attitudes. However, Brooke's assessment proved all too correct. The German Blitzkrieg when it came shattered the French and Belgian forces. Luckily, Brooke and his subordinate Montgomery had secretly planned for just such an eventuality and the two Commanders executed a series of quite brilliant pre-planned manoeuvres to withdraw their troops to the beaches of Dunkirk, where they would be rescued by a flotilla of naval and civilian craft. Brooke was ordered off the beaches ahead of most of his men on May 29th 1940, and left with tears streaming down his face after handing II Corps over to Montgomery. He said he *'felt like a deserter'.*

By June 12th, he was back in France to take command of the 150,000 British troops still in France west of the Seine. It was obvious to Brooke that the French Army was defeated and that it was necessary to evacuate these forces too. This led to his first ever conversation with Churchill, over a crackling and frequently breaking line from France. It turned into a half hour argument. Churchill wanted the British troops hurled splendidly at the advancing Germans and virtually accused Brooke of 'having cold feet' , while Brooke confessed that he was 'on the verge of losing my temper' with the man. Finally Churchill gave in. The troops came home.

Brooke later recalled:

'I had never met Churchill at that time, but even at that distance and through this faulty line, I was at once aware of his dynamic personality and of his dominating influence. It was a useful experience as it gave me an insight into the influence that his magnetic personality might exercise on Commanders at distance'

Britain itself was now under threat of almost immediate invasion. Brooke was promoted to GOC-in-C Home Forces, taking over the post from General Ironside. Unlike his predecessor, who favoured a largely static coastal defence strategy, Brooke developed a mobile reserve to take the battle to the enemy before they could break out of their beach heads. He confessed that he was far from sure of his forces and talked of the 'nakedness of our defences' during the summer of 1940. He also confessed later that he had every intention of using Mustard Gas on the invading troops, should they come.

Eighteen months later, Churchill was seriously despairing of his Chief of the Imperial General Staff (CIGS), General Dill, and was casting about for someone to replace him. Brooke came highly recommended for the top job, but Churchill had serious doubts. He knew that Brooke would be trouble...

'I know these Brookes ... stiff-necked Ulstermen, and there's no-one worse to deal with than that!'

However, he had very little choice. In December 1941 Brooke was appointed CIGS. This essentially meant he was now head of the British Army. Brooke was much admired by his fellow officers and General Alexander probably best summed up the reaction to Brooke's becoming CIGS:

'In his appointment the Prime Minister made a wise choice. I served under (Brooke) as a Commander in the field most of the war and I could not have had a wiser, firmer, or more understanding military chief to guide and look after our interests....'Brookie, as we always call him, was the outstanding and obvious man for the job; a fine soldier in every sense, and trusted and admired by the whole Army.'

The news was broken to Brooke at one of Churchill's weekend getaways at Chequers. Churchill was obviously aware that Brooke was somewhat nervous about assuming the role. Brooke recalled:

'Nobody could be nicer than he (Churchill) was, and finally, when we went to bed at 2am, he came with me into my bedroom to get away from the others, took my hand, and looking into my eyes with an exceptionally kindly look, said, 'I wish you the very best of luck'.

Brooke settled uneasily into the role of CIGS and the extraordinary demands it made upon a man. The need for man-management skills in particular caught him by surprise and he bemoaned:

'Running a war seems to consist in making plans and then ensuring that all those destined to carry it out don't quarrel with each other instead of the enemy.'

And privately he confided to one of his brigadiers:

'This is a frightful thing. I don't know how to tackle it'.

Difficult as the task was, it was nothing compared to the daunting job of managing his Prime Minister. Churchill's sudden bright ideas terrified him and he saw it as his primary role to stop the Prime Minister from doing anything disastrous or mad. Churchill, he believed privately 'knows no details (and) talks absurdities.' The man was, in Brooke's own words, nothing less than 'a public menace'. It took all of Brooke's strength to stand up to Churchill, but stand up he did - again and again and again until he was both exhausted and exasperated.

Churchill meddled constantly, in everything. He meddled with strategy. He meddled with High Command. He was, Brooke saw, rude and aggressive, sulky and inconsistent. Churchill was almost the polar opposite of Brooke in many ways. He was romantic, undisciplined, impulsive, a heavy drinker, a glutton, a wild man, a night owl who kept ridiculous hours - and an individual with little or no sense of his own startling state of semi-nudity. Brooke later wrote in his diary that Churchill combined:

'...genius mixed with an astonishing lack of vision – he is quite the most difficult man to work with that I have ever struck but I should not have missed the chance of working with him for anything on earth!'

The arguments were frequent and explosive. Brooke would look Churchill right in the eye and say, 'I flatly disagree'. While they fought, Brooke was known to break his pencil in half in sheer frustration. When Churchill had gone, Brooke even took to mimicking him behind his back to the delight of other senior officers. It was a true love-hate relationship – for both men. Churchill secretly admired Brooke for having the guts to stand up to him, recalling:

'When I thump the table and push my face towards him what does he do? Thumps the table harder and glares back at me.'

In 1942, Brooke had to discover new reserves of diplomacy and skill within himself to dampen American enthusiasm for a D-Day in 1942 (then called Operation Sledgehammer). He liked Roosevelt, recording in his diary 'I was much impressed by him – a most attractive personality,' and was respectful of his American counterpart General Marshall. When Marshall told him that he sometimes didn't see Roosevelt for six weeks, Brooke replied that he considered himself lucky if he didn't see Churchill for six hours!

Early in that year, Brooke received an unexpected opportunity to escape from the fearful task of having to control Churchill and the impetuous American military, and to return to a more familiar soldier's life. He was offered the job of Commander of British forces in the Middle East. It was a grand opportunity in the most vital theatre of the war at the time – but Brooke turned it down. He agonised but in the end he realised he was just too afraid of what Churchill might do if he wasn't there to keep him in check. Brooke had developed a coping strategy - that of pouring his secret thoughts out into the daily diary which he kept for his wife – and against regulations. Now he wrote:

'One of the most difficult days of my life. I had been offered the finest command I could ever hope for and I turned it down. It would take at least six months for any successor, taking over from me, to become as familiar with Churchill and his ways. During these six months anything might happen.'

So the war continued – and as did the war between Churchill and Brooke. After one particularly bad falling out between the two men, General Ismay tried to play the role of peacemaker. Churchill told him he thought his working relationship with Brooke was finally over because *'he hates me. I can see hatred looking from his eyes.'* When Ismay told Brooke this, the Ulsterman replied, *'Hate him? I don't hate him. I love him. But the first time I tell him that I agree with him when I don't will be the time to get rid of me, for then I can be no more use to him.'* Ismay, playing go-between, told Churchill of Brooke's response and a tearful Prime Minister just sighed,*'dear Brookie..'*

Brooke's other coping strategy was to escape from the War Rooms between meetings and wander all over central London browsing in second hand and antiquarian bookshops for rare and precious books about birds. He was a dedicated ornithologist and it kept him sane.

In 1943, Brooke decided that the war was going sufficiently well that he could move on, at least fairly secure in the knowledge that Churchill couldn't do much harm now when left to his own devices. Churchill had, apparently, promised Brooke the job of Commander of the Allied invasion of Western Europe. When the post went to American General George C. Marshall after the first Quebec Conference, Brooke was deeply hurt and even further offended by Churchill's lack of interest in his feelings and general dismissiveness. *'(He) dealt with the matter as if it were one of minor importance',* Brooke recalled bitterly in his diary. *'Not for one moment did he realise what this meant to me.'*

Brooke was stuck now as CIGS. He was promoted to Field Marshal in January 1944 – and Churchill was still driving him mad right up to the very end as the war entered its final days. On April 12th, he recorded in his diary:

'We had to consider this morning one of Winston's worst minutes I have ever seen. I can only believe that he must have been quite tight when he dictated it. My God! How little the world at large knows what his failings and defects are!'

On 7th May 1945 with victory secured, Brooke wrote in his diary, *'I can't feel thrilled, my main sensation is one of infinite mental weariness.'* A day later – on V.E. Day itself - he complained in his diary that Churchill had never promoted his Chiefs of Staff to the press nor even spoken well of them to the public. They remained, he considered, largely unrecognised and unheralded.

Brooke was created Baron Alanbrooke, of Brookeborough in the County of Fermanagh, in 1945 and Viscount Alanbrooke in 1946 for

CIRCA 1942: General Sir Alan Brooke looking pensive at his desk in the War Office in London

his war service. He retired from the British Army in 1946, became Honorary Colonel Commandant of the Honourable Artillery Company, and pursued business interests in banking and oil. It was not to be a comfortable retirement. Money was a problem, and he and his wife had to move into the gardener's cottage on their estate in Hartley Wintney, Hampshire. They were also forced to sell many of Brooke's rare bird books from his collection, built up over the war years.

The publication of Churchill's 'The Second World War' infuriated Brooke. He thought Churchill wanted to give the impression that he alone had won the war and had ignored the vital part played by his generals. Something had to be done to set the record straight – and so Brooke decided to publish his secret wartime diaries in two volumes - 'The Turn of the Tide' and 'Triumph in the West'. Even in a strongly censored form, the diaries were incendiary. His comments on working with Churchill were a revelation – but many of his other expressed views were sensational too. The diaries would contain kind words for American General McArthur and Field Marshal Sir John Dill, but he referred to Field Marshal Lord Alexander as 'unintelligent' and said that both Eisenhower and Marshall were poor strategists. Brooke's diaries were first published in a heavily abridged and censored form in 1957 and 1959, but were still enough to greatly upset Churchill. Shortly after publication, Churchill pointedly turned his back on Brooke at a party. The full, uncensored text was not released until 2001, when they caused a further furore.

Having made his point, Brooke continued on leading a largely private life. The family was blighted with tragedy in later years. Brooke's daughter Kathleen was killed in a riding accident in 1961 and his wife Benita was killed in a car accident in May 1968. Brooke himself died on June 17th 1963 of a heart attack. His funeral was held at Windsor and he is buried in St Mary's churchyard, near his home in Hartley Wintney. His statue stands today outside the Ministry of Defence in Whitehall, flanked by statues of Montgomery and Slim.

On his plinth it reads, 'Master of Strategy'.

'Pug Ismay, whose contribution to our victory could never be properly rewarded.'
Admiral King

'(Churchill is) not in the least like anyone that you or I have ever met'
General Ismay

They called him Pug, because he looked like one.

1945: General Sir Hastings Ismay at the Potsdam Conference in Germany

ISMAY - THE RELUCTANT CIVIL SERVANT

Hastings Lionel Ismay was born in India on June 21st 1887, the son of a British dignitary on the Viceroy's Legislative Council. He was sent back home to England for schooling at Charterhurst, with the view to him entering Cambridge and becoming a civil servant. Sadly for those ambitions, he did not achieve sufficiently good school results to get into Cambridge and had to make do with attending Sandhurst Military College instead. He was pleased to have failed. He'd always secretly dreamed of being a dashing cavalry officer rather than a dull civil servant.

After leaving Sandhurst, he served a year's apprenticeship with the Gloucestershire infantry regiment in India before eventually finding a place with the 21st Prince Albert Victor's Own Cavalry in 1907. Life with the cavalry, he later recalled was 'blissful'. He chased Mohmand Afghan raiders, rescued kidnapped Hindu women from rapacious Mohammadans and eventually fell over with heatstroke.

Ismay was in Africa when the First World War broke out, serving as second in command of the Somaliland Camel Corps. He begged high command to transfer him to the Western Front, but he was deemed too important to leave Africa. Instead, he spent most of 1914 chasing Mohammed Abdullah Hassan – or 'The Mad Mullah' as the British called him (not to be confused with 'the Mad Mahdi'.) Hassan had been a thorn in the side of colonial authorities for over 20 years and there were now ambitious plans to deal with him once and for all. Ismay took part in the assault on Hassan's stronghold on top of Shimber Berris, the tallest peak in Somalia – but then orders arrived telling the British forces not to engage in any more offensives. The first few months of the Great War had led to shocking losses in the British Army and the military were not keen on frittering away valuable men chasing a religious lunatic with no gain for the real war effort.

Ismay was still with the Camel Corps in Somaliland in January 1920, when the British Army finally felt strong enough to go after Hassan once again. Ismay led the Camel Corps in an assault on another of Hassan's strongholds, this time at Jidali. As his men fought a ferocious defensive action, the Mad Mullah slipped out of the fortress with part of his forces under cover of night. Ismay went after him, capturing many members of his family including seven of his sons – but never could find the Mullah. He remained in hiding from the British until the end of 1920, when he very conveniently died of Spanish Flu.

By that time, Ismay was already back in England. He had been sickened by the scale of the carnage of the First World War and was seriously thinking about leaving the military. In April 1921, Ismay married his fiancée, Laura Clegg. The couple would eventually have three daughters. In the 1930s, Laura would enjoy a series of inheritances, leaving Ismay rather wealthy. He returned to India the same year as he married and eventually attended Staff College in Rawalpindi before becoming deputy assistant

quartermaster general of the Indian Army with Claude Auchinleck. He didn't like the work. It was too much like being a civil servant. Perhaps that's just what he was fated to be. In a strange twist of fate, he ended up next attending the RAF Staff College in Andover and emerged from there to gain a post as assistant secretary of the Committee of Imperial Defence. He was now effectively a civil servant by any other name.

Now a Colonel, Ismay returned to India in December 1930 with dreams of changing the direction of his life and taking charge of an elite Indian Cavalry Regiment. Instead, he got another civil service job, this time as military secretary to the Viceroy. His days of chasing wild Mohmand raiders were, it seemed, well and truly over and he began to accept it. By 1933, he was back in England again, serving as an intelligence officer with the War Office under Major General Dill. 1936 saw Ismay promoted to deputy secretary of the Committee of Imperial Defence. War with Germany now seemed 'imminent' to Ismay, and he threw himself into the task of helping

DECEMBER 1944: Portrait of General Sir Hastings Ismay

to build the nation's defences with vigour. He became secretary of the Committee of Imperial Defence on August 1st 1938 and - while Prime Minister Neville Chamberlain was in Munich visiting and placating Hitler - , Ismay caused a stir by ordering air raid defences trenches to be dug in London. He fully expected war, and privately believed that Chamberlain should have declared war in 1938 rather than making any more attempts at appeasement.

When war broke out, Ismay was promoted to Major-General and found himself working closely with Chamberlain, although he had strong doubts about the Prime Minister's military acumen. When Churchill took over the Military Co-ordination Committee in May 1940, Ismay was selected to serve as his chief staff officer – and was absolutely delighted He would later write that Churchill was nothing less than 'the greatest Englishman of his time, perhaps of all time'. Chamberlain resigned. Churchill became both Prime Minister and Minister of Defence – and began to rely on Ismay more and more. *'We became hand in glove, and much more',* Churchill later recalled. Ismay described his role as 'my chief's shadow' and the chief as 'Superman.' He also confessed that if Churchill ever wanted to wipe his boots on him, he'd let him – such was his admiration for the man.

Ismay was appointed deputy secretary of the War Cabinet and Churchill found him invaluable as a bridge between the civilian and military leadership. Most of all, Ismay used all of his *'tact, patience, and skill'* (as Churchill's private secretary Jock Colville put it) trying to keep Churchill and his military chiefs from not going to war against each other.

Although he was there chiefly as a military advisor, Ismay also found his diplomatic skills essential as he accompanied Churchill to important foreign summits. He forged friendly personal relations with President Eisenhower (who called him a man of 'great ability') and helped to smooth out difficult Anglo-American relations on a number of occasions.

By 1944, Ismay was deeply involved with the planning of Operation Overlord, especially the deception elements designed to confuse the Germans about where and when the landings would come. He was promoted to full General in May of 1944 and, after the success of the D-Day landings, was personally selected by King George VI to accompany His Majesty on a visit to the troops.

Ismay's position as an insider at many of the major wartime international conferences had led him to worry about the nature of the post-war world and he was still unhappy when V.E. Day came. The Nazis may have been defeated, he saw, but Stalin's iron empire was stronger than ever and had ranged deep into Europe. Ismay had intended to retire on VJ Day but government work kept him busy until 1947. Ever the loyal servant, Ismay did what was required of him. Finally, Ismay resigned from Clement Attlee's government and was created a baron - Baron Ismay, of Wormington in the County of Gloucester. He looked forward to a retirement well spent in the House of Lords. It was not to be.

In early 1947, Lord Mountbatten was appointed Viceroy of India. Ismay volunteered to join him as Chief of Staff and help smooth the path to Indian Independence. Both men dreamed of a united, independent India but it soon became all-too-apparent that this would never happen because of the seething religious hatred between Moslem and Hindu . 'India was a ship on fire in mid-ocean with ammunition in her hold,' Ismay said, summing up the position they found themselves in. Both men quickly abandoned their original plans and worked instead towards independence – and Partition. Mountbatten got Ismay to sell the plan to the British government.

After the complexities and horrors of Partition, the job of Chairman of the Council of the Festival of Britain must have seemed like nothing to Ismay. He took the job as a favour to Churchill and it was Churchill who brought Ismay out of retirement for a second time to serve as the Secretary of State for Commonwealth relations in Churchill's 1951 government. Although he thought the fledgling NATO was a mess, he became the organisation's first Secretary General. He'd originally said no, but Churchill had persuaded him as only Churchill could.

Ismay left NATO in late 1956, insisting that it needed a *'fresh hand and a fresh brain'*. He settled down to write his rather kindly memoirs and to pursue some business interests but was called upon one final time in 1963, to review the organisation of the British military for the M.O.D. Hastings Ismay died on December 17th 1965 at his home in Gloucestershire. He was 78 years old.

'..in Monty we certainly had a soldier who knew his onions, no matter what the "high-ups" in the army might officially think of the smell.'

Sir Arthur Harris

'In defeat, unbeatable; in victory, unbearable.'

Winston Churchill

'In dealing with him one must remember that he is not quite a gentleman.'

Field Marshal Lord Gort

'..he is liable to commit untold errors in lack of tact'

Brooke

Churchill once said that it was not just the *'good boys'* who help to win wars. *'It is the sneaks and stinkers as well'.* Bernard Montgomery was a sneak and a stinker. Indeed, they called him at lot worse. This was not a nice man. During World War One, he had captured a German prisoner by the distinctly ungentlemanly tactic of kneeing him vigorously and enthusiastically in the groin. General Sir Bernard Freyberg, of the New Zealand Army once called Montgomery a *'little bastard'* but refined his comment by uttering that, *'If Montgomery is a cad, it's a great pity that the British Army doesn't have a few more bounders.'*

It was General Ismay who first warned Churchill of Montgomery's 'eccentricities'. Rather than putting Churchill off, it piqued his curiosity. Churchill went down to meet Montgomery in the summer of 1940 and the two ended up having dinner in a Brighton hotel. Churchill found Montgomery a strange customer. He was just five foot seven tall with hawkish features and piercing blue eyes. When he spoke, his voice was screechy and strangely high pitched. Whatever Churchill made of his physical presence that night, he was most certainly quite horrified that his dinner companion was not drinking.

'Never touch the stuff!' Montgomery said forcefully. *'Don't drink, don't smoke – and I'm one hundred per cent fit!'.* Churchill stared at him as if he were from the planet Mars and then retorted, *'Well, I drink as much brandy as I can get and I smoke cigars and I'm two hundred per cent fit!'*

Montgomery later wrote: *'I have never discovered what Churchill thought of me that day; I know I was immensely impressed by him'.*

MONTGOMERY - THE OUTSIDER

Bernard Law Montgomery was born into a large and passionately religious family in Kennington, London, on November 17th 1887. His father was the vicar of St. Mark's in Kennington and his mother Maud was the daughter of a noted Canterbury preacher. He was the fourth of nine children. Although the Montgomery's were Irish-Scots gentry, money was tight.

Two years after Montgomery was born his father, Henry, was appointed Bishop of Tasmania and the whole family relocated down under. Henry spent much of his time in Tasmania away from home preaching in far-flung corners of the island and Maud filled her otherwise empty days by viciously beating her young children or else neglecting them. By all accounts, she hated Montgomery so deeply that she essentially abandoned him.

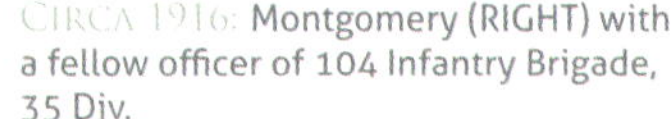
CIRCA 1916: Montgomery (RIGHT) with a fellow officer of 104 Infantry Brigade, 35 Div.

22ND JUNE 1943: King George VI with General Montgomery at Eighth Army HQ, TRIPOLI

30TH SEPTEMBER 1943: General Montgomery is handed a scarf by his batman, Corp. W English, in camp at Eighth Army Headquarters, Italy

Montgomery was allowed to run wild and became something of a little bully, terrorising the other children. *'I was a dreadful little boy. I don't suppose anybody would put up with my sort of behaviour these days,'* he recalled later. The bad behaviour continued when the family returned to London in 1901. After attending St Paul's School (where he was judged 'weak' in the academic department and nicknamed 'monkey' for his wild behaviour on the football pitch), Montgomery went on to the Royal Military College at Sandhurst, where he was very nearly expelled for bad behaviour (including sword fighting with red hot pokers) and acts of violence (such as setting fire to the shirt tails of a fellow officer, giving him third degree burns). His place at Sandhurst was only saved by his mother, who begged the C.O. to reconsider expulsion because *'Bernard is not fit to be anything more than a soldier'.*

On graduating from Sandhurst in 1908, Montgomery received a commission and joined The Royal Warwickshire Regiment of infantry at the rank of second Lieutenant. He was still with them war broke out in 1914. He was shipped to Europe with the British Expeditionary Force and saw action almost immediately during the retreat from Mons. On October 13th 1914, he led a platoon of men on a bayonet charge against a German trench and was shot through the chest and knee by a sniper. When Montgomery was returned to his lines by stretcher party, his wounds were thought so severe that he had no chance of surviving. A grave was dug for him in preparation but somehow Montgomery pulled through. For his bravery he was awarded a D.S.O. while recuperating in England. His health finally restored, Montgomery returned to the Western Front as a Brigade Major in 1916, and fought with the 33rd Division at the Battle of Arras in Spring 1917. Later that year he fought at the Battle of Passchendaele. By the end of the war he was ranked as a temporary Lieutenant-Colonel and was to all intents and purposes Chief of Staff of the 47th (2nd London) Division. Looking back at the war in his memoirs, he was typically blunt:

'The frightful casualties appalled me. The so-called 'good fighting generals' of the war appeared to me to be those who had a complete disregard for human life.'

Montgomery swore that, were he ever in the same position, he would not treat his men in such a cavalier fashion. Whatever his other faults, it was a promise he kept.

After the Great War ended, it seemed that Montgomery's career might end too. He was not selected for Staff College. But then fate intervened. He just happened to meet the Commander-in-Chief of the British Army of Occupation, Sir William Robertson at a tennis party, and was able to sweet talk him into letting him in. Following Staff College – and newly promoted now to Brigade Major – Montgomery joined the 17th Infantry Brigade in 1921 and took part in counter insurgency operations against Irish Nationalists. He thought fighting them was futile. In his opinion, Oliver Cromwell or the Germans could have dealt with the rebels, but the brutality required to win the day would never be approved by the British public.

Montgomery met Elizabeth Carver, a widower with children, whilst

1st February 1944: Meeting of the Supreme Command, Allied Expeditionary Force, London

12th June 1944: Major-General Maxwell Taylor, 101st (US) Airborne Division receives the DSO from Montgomery for gallantry in action

21st July 1944: General Montgomery with Winston Churchill

skiing in Switzerland in 1926 . They married in 1927 and their son David was born the following year. An aspiring artist, Elizabeth had many friends from the arts world and they were horrified by this military man who couldn't it seemed speak about anything except war. The word 'philistine' got thrown around. She didn't care. For his part, Montgomery must have been thoroughly confused by his new role as husband and tried to treat their home as a barracks. He would post signs saying 'Orders of the Day' on the dining room door with such bullet points as 'Lunch at 13.00 hrs.' Elizabeth just ignored it all.

By 1931, he was a Lieutenant-Colonel commanding the 1st Battalion of The Royal Warwickshire Regiment and saw service in Palestine and India. He became a Full Colonel in 1934 and then an instructor at the Indian Army Staff College in Quetta. Montgomery returned to Britain in June 1937 as a temporary Brigadier. That same year, he lost his wife. The couple were holidaying in Burnham-on-Sea when Elizabeth was bitten by an insect. The bite quickly became infected and she passed away from septicaemia. On his return from his wife's funeral, Montgomery wrote:

'The funeral is over. I sat in the room at the hospital until they came to screw the lid on the coffin. I kissed her dear face for the last time just before the lid was put on. I tried hard to bear up at the service and at the graveside. But I could not bear it and I am afraid I broke down utterly. I feel desperately lonely and sad. I suppose in time I shall get over it, but at present it seems that I never shall.'

Returning to the Army was difficult, but he did pull himself together. After being promoted to Major-General in 1938, Montgomery took command of the 8th Infantry Division in Palestine and quashed an Arab rebellion, a fight which he later said he enjoyed. By 1939, he was home again, now commanding the 3rd (Iron) Infantry Division. He was a hard taskmaster for his troops, insisting on a continuous regime of training, manoeuvres and P.E. – and not just his troops but his senior officers too. One staff colonel complained that, if he were ordered to run seven miles like the others in 3rd Division, he would surely die of heart failure. Montgomery replied, *'Good. If you're going to die, die now – so we can get a fit replacement by the time the battle starts!'*

Montgomery's 3rd Division shipped out to France as part of the British Expeditionary Force. When the German Blitzkrieg came in May 1940, Montgomery executed a series of brilliant manoeuvres as 3rd Division disengaged from close contact with the enemy and retreated to Dunkirk. His senior Commander, General Brooke, recorded in his diary;

'Found (Montgomery) had, as usual, accomplished the impossible.'

When Brooke was recalled to London and taken off the beaches, he passed temporary command of II Corps to Montgomery. His men were successfully evacuated from the beach with minimal casualties – but Montgomery himself was furious. Once home in London, he hurled a tirade of abuse at the War Office about the

quality of command of the BEF that won him few friends – and an effective side-lining as he was reassigned to divisional command for his sins.

However, good able Commanders were thin on the ground and by July of 1940 he was made an acting Lieutenant-General and given command of V Corps, which was responsible for the defence of Hampshire and Dorset. It wasn't long before he started to fight with those above him again, this time sparking a long-running animosity with General Auchinleck, the new Commander-in-Chief, Southern Command. He would stay at home now until mid-1942, when he became Commander of the British 8th Army – the famous 'Desert Rats' - by a stroke of fate. General Gott was to assume charge of the 8th Army but had been killed when his plane was shot down on route to Cairo. It was CIGS General Brooke's idea to replace Gott with Montgomery, who had only just been appointed as Commander of the British ground forces for the forthcoming Operation Torch. Montgomery packed up and left.

Upon his arrival in Egypt in mid-August 1942, Montgomery hit the 8th Army like a whirlwind, demanding much from a thoroughly demoralised and generally not well regarded force. He reorganised them into separate tank and infantry units (which was definitely not seen as the way to do things), patched up defensive lines, called up two British Divisions which had only just arrived in Egypt and started working on plans to better co-ordinate air, sea and land operations. Moreover, he destroyed every copy of the contingency plans the British had for retreat should Rommel come against them in force. At his very first meeting with his new officers, he told them:

'I have cancelled the plan for withdrawal. If we are attacked, then there will be no retreat. If we cannot stay here alive, then we will stay here dead.'

This was not the kind of thinking his officers were used to – but his self-confidence was infectious. This was a man who after all, when asked which three generals he admired most replied 'the other two would be Alexander the Great and Napoleon.'

Montgomery made a point of touring his troops, addressing them vigorously and bribing them with cigarettes. He took note of their concerns – the quality of their food, the poor state of the latrines and problems with sending and receiving mail – and did something about it. He told them;

'I want to impose on everyone that the bad times are over, they are finished! Our mandate from the Prime Minister is to destroy the Axis forces in North Africa...It can be done, and it will be done!

The effect was almost immediate. His men took to him straight away. He was direct, confident – and just eccentric enough to be endearing without being in danger of thought mad. Although he had access to a large and luxurious house for his personal use, he preferred to live in a caravan in its garden (wherein he kept a picture of Rommel) – and his men knew it too. When Brooke and Alexander came to visit just a week after Montgomery had taken command, they were astounded by the effect he had already had on the 8th.

On August 31st, Rommel attacked at Alam Halfa. The fighting was ferocious but the 8th held and Rommel retreated again. Montgomery was criticised for not launching an immediate counter attack – but he was just biding his time, waiting for the moment when he had all the resources he needed in place. Churchill, naturally, got fidgety at the lack of progress and sent Montgomery's superior, Alexander, a tart telegram on September 23rd saying 'We are in your hands and of course a victorious battle makes amends for much delay.' Alexander at the time was struggling to control Montgomery as he later wrote in his memoirs:

'...I can't disguise that he was not an easy man to deal with; for example, administrative orders issued by my staff were sometimes objected to - in other words Monty wanted to have complete independence of command and to do what he liked. '

Montgomery gives an indication of what he must have been like to deal with in his war diary:

'My first day in the desert had been a very good one, though long and tiring. I'm afraid that it was with an insubordinate smile that I fell asleep: I was issuing orders to an army which someone else reckoned he commanded!'

Montgomery was still waiting, for the extra tanks he needed, for his men to be properly trained in night fighting and mine clearance... and for his schedule to allow him to personally visit every single

NOVEMBER 1942: General Bernard L. Montgomery watches his tanks move up in North Africa

CIRCA 1944: Montgomery as he is appointed Colonel Commandant of the Parachute Regiment

CIRCA 1944: Bernard Montgomery in pensive mood

15TH JANUARY 1945: Montgomery wearing the jump jacket and red beret of the Parachute Regiment

one of his men, of whom there were now 231,000 assembled in the desert. Rommel – and Churchill – could wait.

Rommel was not in the Western Desert when Montgomery finally decided to strike at El Alamein on October 23rd. He was in hospital in Germany. He had to race back when his temporary replacement - General Stumme – keeled over and died of a heart attack just a few hours into the battle. But even Rommel couldn't stop the 8th Army this time. Churchill for his part was having dinner with Eleanor Roosevelt at Buckingham Palace when he heard the news of the long awaited attack. He responded with a vigorous celebratory performance of 'Roll Out the Barrel.'

After the largest continuous artillery barrage seen since the First World War, Allied armour and infantry smashed through the German and Italian lines over the course of 12 days and soon the enemy was in full retreat along the coast road with Allied forces in hot pursuit. The chase was only stopped by a violent and intense rainstorm. Montgomery had to force back tears of rage as he reluctantly called off the pursuit, his tanks and armoured cars becoming bogged down.

The Battle of El Alamein was still an overwhelming Allied victory. Over 30,000 Axis prisoners were taken including Rommel's second-in-command, General von Thoma and the Germans lost in excess of 450 tanks and 1,000 artillery pieces. Churchill was delighted and ordered church bells to ring out throughout Britain to mark the occasion. 'Before Alamein we never had a victory,' he said. 'After Alamein we never had a defeat.' It was also his inspiration to say famously on November 10th:

'This is not the end. It is not even the beginning of the end. But it is, perhaps, the end of the beginning.'

He also, rather ungenerously said, *'Pity our first victorious general should be a bounder of the first water...'*

Tripoli fell to the Allies on January 23rd. Montgomery was promoted to full General and resumed the pursuit, driving the Afrika Korps out every time they tried to establish new defensive lines. The last Axis forces in North Africa surrendered in Tunisia on May 11th. The 8th Army were rewarded with a brothel in Libya, personally approved by Montgomery. Brother officers tutted. Montgomery now found himself a national hero. Returning to London, he would find himself mobbed whenever he went out in public. He loved it.

With the Axis smashed in North Africa, Allied attention now turned to Sicily. Montgomery, typically, took one look at the plans of the invasion of Sicily drawn up by General Alexander and General Eisenhower – and told them they were unworkable. They were, he said *'a dog's breakfast which broke every common sense rule of practical fighting'.* Despite his astounding arrogance, he got his way. The invasion plans were duly redrawn and the resulting revised combat operation was judged an outstanding success. However, Montgomery was now the source of considerable tension between the British and Americans. Both General

20TH MARCH 1945: Montgomery acknowledges the cheers of Belgian civilians during a tour of 5th Division, Ghent

MARCH 1945: Montgomery with Major General Simpson inspect the 'Dragon's Teeth' part of the Siegfried Line

MARCH 1945: Montgomery with Churchill and General Simpson, on blown bridge at Wesel

Patton and General Bradley had their noses put out of joint by Montgomery's boastful arrogance and Patton later went as far as to call Montgomery a *'tired little fart'*. Bradley criticised Montgomery's scruffy appearance, saying that he looked like nothing so much as *'a poorly tailored bohemian painter.'*

Montgomery continued to lead the 8th Army as they landed in Italy and fought their way north. However he was appalled by the chaos of the Italian Campaign and its lack of co-ordination and cooperation between British and American forces. He again called it a 'Dog's Breakfast' and made no secret of the fact he was relieved to finally leave the theatre during Christmas 1943.

Montgomery was now on his way back to Britain to take charge of the 21st Army Group – which comprised all the Allied ground forces to be used for the forthcoming invasion of Normandy. He was now effectively second only to the Supreme Commander, Allied Expeditionary Forces, American General Eisenhower. He presented his plans for the invasion and the 90 day campaign to follow at his old school – St Pauls – and the innovations he introduced including an increase in divisional strength and the number of beach heads to be attacked proved critical to the success of D-Day. He also made a point of touring the country and speaking to as many of his troops as possible, as he had before El Alamein.

Following D-Day, Montgomery remained in charge of Allied ground forces until September 1st 1944, when Eisenhower took over from him, leaving Montgomery to look after British and Canadian troops in theatre. Although this had all been planned and agreed in advance, Montgomery was nevertheless bitterly offended by what he saw as a demotion. Churchill had him promoted to Field Marshal as a way of soothing his feelings.

Montgomery refused to play a back seat role and still managed to persuade Eisenhower on the merits of Operation Market Garden. Market Garden was a bold and aggressive plan – reckless even – and very atypical of the kind of tactics Montgomery usually subscribed to. Designed to shorten the war, it involved dropping British and Polish paratroopers into the Dutch town of Arnhem to secure a vital bridge across the River Rhine while American forces would race to join them, crossing several heavily defended river crossings in the course of their advance. During the planning, Montgomery almost fell out with Eisenhower, by lecturing the general as if he were a child: *'Steady Monty,'* Eisenhower had to say. *'You cannot talk to me like this. I am your boss.'* Montgomery backed down. Market Garden failed. The paratroopers dropped on Arnhem found themselves right in the midst of an elite German tank unit (the 2nd S.S. Panzer Corps) being refitted, while the column racing to join up with them became bogged down in relentless, heavy fighting. The casualties were severe.

Montgomery was fortunate in that his now damaged reputation was restored somewhat during the Battle of the Bulge that December, when the Germans unleashed their armoured reserve in a massive counter-attack that smashed into American forces in the Ardennes Forest. The American response was piecemeal and chaotic. Eisenhower transferred control of the American units to Montgomery, who was physically closest to the battle. It may have greatly upset General Bradley and his sense of American national pride, but it worked. Montgomery managed to pull the various fighting forces together and get them working in a tight coordinated fashion to a dedicated battle plan. The German advance was halted and turned back on itself.

On March 24th 1945, Montgomery's 21st Army Group crossed the Rhine and quickly helped to encircle and trap the German Army Group B in the Ruhr. On May 4th, Montgomery personally took the Surrender of German forces in north-west Germany, Denmark and the Netherlands. He then commanded British occupation forces and the Army of the Rhine and made some exceptional efforts to help the burdens of the shattered Germans. He told his soldiers to smile at the children and to be nice to them. He encouraged a free press and worked to try and use the influence of the church to help detoxify the nation from the poison of Nazism.

After V.E. Day, Field Marshal Brooke was involved in some intense discussions about who would succeed him as CIGs. Montgomery's name came up. Everyone thought he would be very good in the role, but that he made too many enemies amongst British officers (not to mention their American allies) and his lack of tact would cause serious and perhaps fatal friction. They were spot on. 1st Viscount Montgomery of Alamein, as Montgomery had been created in 1946, did succeed Brooke as CIGS and his three years in the role from 1946-1948 was considered near disastrous. He fell out so badly with some of his fellow chiefs that they would barely speak to him, or he to them. Things got so fractious that he wouldn't even turn up for meetings, preferring to send his deputies instead. He had few friends in politics either. When he tried to nominate John Crocker as his own successor as CIGS, the Prime Minister Clement Attlee overruled him. *'I've already told him, '* Montgomery said, to which Attlee replied *'Untell him.'*

Things went little better when Montgomery was made Chairman of the Western European Union's Commanders-in-Chief committee. He fell out spectacularly with his French land forces chief, causing the entire organisation HQ to split along partisan lines. Escaping from the chaos he was at least partly responsible for, Montgomery next became Eisenhower's deputy in forging NATO's European forces. He served in this capacity from 1951 to 1958, excelling at the military aspects of his task but all at sea with the diplomacy.

Montgomery finally retired in 1958. He devoted himself to the Winkle Club (a noted charity) and to boy's schools including St. John's School in Leatherhead, Surrey and to the Viscount Montgomery School in Ontario, Canada, which was named in his honour.

He continued to get into trouble. When his war memoirs appeared, they were full of abuse of his fellow Commanders. Eisenhower, he thought, had prolonged the war by a year through poor leadership. (Eisenhower at this time was now President Eisenhower, the most powerful man in the free world, and didn't take kindly to Montgomery's views. Their friendship ended somewhat abruptly.) What's more Field-Marshal Auchinleck threatened to sue him for suggesting that Auchinleck's grand plans to deal with Rommel had in reality been a plan for retreat. Montgomery was forced to publically apologise on a radio broadcast. He also stated that anyone who voted Labour should be locked up.

In later life, his views became more and more controversial. After a visit to South Africa in 1962, he spoke out in favour of apartheid and after visiting Red China said how impressed he was by the Communist leadership. He supported the beating of children proclaiming, *'I was well beaten myself, and I am better for it.'* (but it should be noted that when his mother Maud died in 1949, Montgomery said he was *'too busy'* to attend her funeral.) He was also a leading opponent of the Sexual Offences Act 1967, which was to legalise homosexuality in Britain. He said, memorably:

'This sort of thing may be tolerated by the French, but we're British – thank God.'

Bernard Law Montgomery died on March 24th 1976 at Isington, near Alton in Hampshire. He was 88 years old. During his lifetime, he had done more than enough to ensure he would be remembered where other British heroes would be largely forgotten. In his later years however, he had almost become a parody of himself, a bitter and bitterly unhappy old man raging at the world around him and devoting himself to his collection of lovebirds. He was lonely, he was mocked – especially by the Left – and he was burgled by thieves who stole many of his most treasured keepsakes. They were never caught and it broke his elderly heart.

Montgomery with his puppies "Hitler" and "Rommel" at his mobile headquarters in Normandy

'..more bluff and brawn than brain.'
Henry Pownall

'I would sum up the German character best by saying that they are the best of losers and the worst of winners.'
Ironside

'War cannot be run by the Staffs sitting around the table arguing. We cannot have a man (Churchill) trying to supervise all the military arrangements as if he were a company Commander running a small operation to cross a bridge.'
Ironside

IRONSIDE - THE BRUISER

General Ironside was a big man. Very big. Six feet four. On his appointment as Commander-in-Chief Home Forces in May 1940, the Ottawa Citizen newspaper referred to him as a '250lb giant of a man'. That was why everyone referred to him as 'Tiny' or 'Big Bill'.

Ironside was also a blunt man, unskilled in diplomacy, and possessed of a ferocious temper if roused. He was also very much a man of his time and of the British Empire. He had his own manservant, enjoyed hunting dangerous big game and hated foreigners with a passion. He also loathed women, politicians, pacifists, university professors and air marshals. In private people – presumably not foreign, female or those employed in the aforementioned professions – found him warm, friendly and honest. Ironside's true passion was for dogs, whom he simply adored, and a succession of them followed him on campaign. Ironside was baffled as to why he made so many enemies in his life, but make enemies he did – and that would determine the course of his military career.

William Edmund Ironside was born in Edinburgh on May 6th 1880. His father was a surgeon-major with the Royal Horse Artillery. When his father died shortly after Ironside's birth, his mother chose to take the boy with her to the continent where the cost of living was considerably less than in Scotland. They travelled widely, and the young boy soon developed an affinity for learning new languages. By the end of his life it's estimated that Ironside had mastered anything up to 17 languages, from French to Urdu.

After returning to Britain and receiving a secondary education at Tonbridge School in Kent, Ironside attended the Royal Military Academy in Woolwich, South London, intending to follow his late father into the Royal Horse Artillery. The RMA was the making of him. Although he had demonstrated skill with languages, he had previously been a distinctly mediocre student in all other subjects. Now, he applied himself to his studies with a new vigour and developed a keen interest in sports. He was an excellent boxer and played rugby not only for the college but also internationally for Scotland.

Ironside received his commission and joined the Royal Horse Artillery in 1899, soon after which he was posted to South Africa and fought in the Second Boer War where he met a young Winston Churchill. After being wounded in action three times, he emerged with a decoration and a promotion to Lieutenant. At the war's end, Ironside undertook a spying mission for Her Majesty's Government under secondment to the Secret Service. Growing a beard and disguising himself as a Boer – he spoke Afrikaans perfectly – Ironside managed to get a job as a wagon driver with the German military in South West Africa and sent back valuable intelligence to Whitehall. He managed to stay undercover for two years, despite almost being caught twice – once

8th September 1939: Ironside arrives at Downing Street, in the first week of World War II, with Marshal of the Royal Air Force Sir Cyril Newall and First Sea Lord, Sir Dudley Pound

Circa 1939: Ironside, at work at his desk

when he made the mistake of answering a German NCO in perfect, educated German and once when he forgot to remove the collar from his faithful dog which had his real name and contact details on it. When questioned, he said he had stolen the dog from the British. So successful was he that, he was even awarded the German Military Medal for his services to the Fatherland.

It was only 40 years later that Ironside discovered his adventures had directly inspired one of the great adventure characters of British literature, when he met a young officer who happened to be John Buchan's son. *'Did you ever know, Sir,'* the young officer said to him, *'that my father John Buchan took you as his model for the character of Richard Hannay?'* Richard Hannay was the hero of three bestselling books, The Thirty-Nine Steps, Greenmantle and Mr. Standfast.

There are stories that Ironside was one of the very first British officers to arrive on the continent as part of the British Expeditionary Force after war broke out in 1914. He arrived as a Captain and was promoted to Major within just a couple of months, joining the 6th Division. In 1915, he was awarded the D.S.O. for 'outstanding bravery'. That same year he married Mariot Ysobel Cheyne. They would have a son and daughter together. In 1916, Ironside was posted to the 4th Canadian Division, where he was required to take charge on a number of occasions. The Division arrived in France just in time to participate in the last part of the Somme campaign and Ironside went on to fight at both Vimy Ridge and Passchendaele. Just three months before the end of the First World War, he suddenly found himself promoted to Brigadier General and given command of the Allied Expeditionary Force which had been despatched to Northern Russia to block a proposed German offensive. The expedition soon turned into an action to fight the Russian Bolsheviks instead. By all accounts, Ironside found himself living like some sort of warlord, laying down the law, settling disputes and signing death warrants. Despite his best efforts, the mission failed and Russia plunged deeper into chaos.

After returning from the east, Ironside spent time in Hungary and in Turkey, intrigued in Persia and found his command of British forces in Iraq interrupted by serious injury following a plane crash. Now Ironside was given command of the Staff College, Camberley. He was to hold the post for four years, running the establishment proficiently whilst fighting against those who believed that military teaching should be based on Great War tactics. After his time at the Staff College, Ironside spent the best part of a decade being bounced from posting to posting by a peacetime army that didn't really know what to do with the surfeit of senior officers in its pay. Finally returning home from India in 1936, Ironside was given responsibility for Eastern Command, which was partly responsible for the Home Defence of Britain should war come. And Ironside knew that war was definitely coming, no matter what the appeasers said. The idea chilled him. 'We are in no state to go to war', he wrote in his diary that year. Ironside did his

CIRCA 1940: Field Marshal Sir Edmund Ironside and Lord Gort studying a map in the War Office, London

9TH MAY 1940: General Sir Edmund Ironside leaving the House of Commons

best to warn of the war to come, and to get Britain better prepared for the inevitable. However these were treacherous times in both political and military circles. His enemies used a lapse in judgement committed during military manoeuvres to blot his copybook and he was passed over as the next Chief of the Imperial General Staff in favour of Lord Gort. This was especially galling to Ironside who held Gort in particularly low esteem.

It seemed like Ironside's enemies had finally won the day and – after a brief period as Aide de Camp to King George - he was exiled from Britain as Governor of Gibraltar. Here, free from the poisonous politics of Whitehall, he set about rapidly improving Gibraltar's military defences and getting it better prepared to withstand a long siege.

Ironside arrived in Gibraltar in November 1938. By December, the powers-that-be suddenly started to see him in a new light. War was coming after all. Everything he had said about modernising the army now desperately needed to happen. And the men at the top were becoming more and more disillusioned with their new CIGS, Lord Gort. Ironside still had powerful enemies, but he was finally offered the post of Inspector-General of Overseas Forces to inspect the readiness of troops outside of the United Kingdom. Although notionally under Gort's command, Ironside treated him with increasing contempt at every opportunity, calling him *'out of his depth'*.

In July 1939, Ironside went to Poland to meet the Polish High Command. He returned with dire warnings. While the Poles were unlikely to provoke Hitler, he said, they could never withstand the German military machine and would be swiftly overrun should war break out. By September 3rd Britain was at war – and Ironside was abruptly appointed as CIGS. It was a complete shock to him. He thought he'd be put in charge of the British Expeditionary Force in France and was already packing to leave. Lord Gort was despatched to France instead. Ironside had been championed as the new CIGS by Churchill at the War Cabinet but even Ironside was unconvinced, admitting *'I am not suited in temperament to such a job as CIGS'.*

Despite his own misgivings, Ironside now worked to build up British Forces in France and in Egypt, an area he'd always anticipated as being vital to the outcome of any future war. However, he was only too aware that he was now directing a British Army that was still too antiquated, too weak and too lacking in modern equipment and armour. It was like starting a game of chess with only half the pieces. He was also regularly upsetting the War Cabinet. Ironside had few diplomatic graces and was considered rather annoying for his bluntness and forcefulness.

For his part, Ironside found the War Cabinet's policy of 'wait and see' enormously frustrating . He referred to Prime Minister Chamberlain as just a 'weary, tired old man' and the other cabinet members as 'mediocrities'. 'Now I'm going to waste a morning educating these old gentlemen on their job,' he once complained.

On April 9th 1940, the Nazis invaded Norway. Ironside had long foreseen this and had plans in place to send British troops to defend Norway's strategically important iron ore fields. As the British troops fought in Norway, Ironside found it almost impossible to get things done, as the War Cabinet became confused and divided, mainly due to Churchill. Churchill, Ironside said, 'bitched' the Norwegian Campaign. It was the beginning of a serious falling out between the two men. In the end, with everyone around him seemingly paralysed, Ironside arranged to have his troops evacuated from Norway. The Germans took the nation.

As the German Blitzkrieg smashed through Belgium and the Netherlands in May 1940, Ironside set off to France to co-ordinate a united Allied response to the crisis. He was very probably the wrong man for the job, as he, generally speaking, despised the French. He found the French Generals utterly confused and demoralised and actually physically attacked General Billotte, grabbing him by his tunic and shaking him. 'The man is completely defeated,' he wrote in his diary later. It was Billotte's job to co-ordinate military action between British, Belgian and French forces in Belgium, but Ironside just ignored him and took over. Naturally the French high command reacted sniffily, with the French Commander-in-Chief, General Weygand, saying that he wanted *'to box Ironside's ears'.* Ironside did manage to co-ordinate action between Gort's BEF and French forces under General Blanchard, but their counterattack at Arras failed. In private Gort and Ironside agreed that the French were finished on the battlefield and that the BEF had to be evacuated at the earliest possible opportunity, although Ironside thought there might be fearful losses during the evacuation. Ironside said to Anthony Eden, then Secretary of War, 'this is the end of the British Empire'. Eden did not disagree.

Ironside came home to find he was to be removed from the post of CIGS and replaced by General Dill. He would instead be appointed Commander-in-Chief, Home Forces and made responsible for the defence of the British Isles. In a way, he was relieved. With the Germans already at Calais, this was a proper task for a soldier and the infighting with Churchill and other politicians had left him fairly sure he was not suited to the post of CIGS.

Now he turned with his customary vigour to his new role. The forces he had available to him for the task were not encouraging - a poorly trained and even more poorly equipped mix of territorials, Home Guard (then called Local Defence Volunteers) and 57 Home Defence Battalions. Ironside saw no way to hold any invasion force on the beaches. They would undoubtedly break through and range inland. His forces would need to manoeuvre to meet them, but they were too poorly trained to be able to do so. Ironside's compromise was to build strong coastal defences, strategically placed pillboxes and forces of mobile artillery hastily mounted on lorries. In the event of invasion, the Germans would be met and held temporarily at the 'defensive crust' on the coast. The second line of defence, located at strategic points inland would be manned by the Home Guard. Fortified 'stop lines' would then attempt to prevent access to London and the Midlands from German units breaking through, while what mobile forces he could muster would meet them as required. It was an unsatisfactory plan – but no one had a better one.

On July 19th, Ironside was summoned to the War Office to be told he was to be replaced immediately by General Brooke as Commander-in-Chief, Home Forces. Behind the scenes Brooke, who did not like Ironside, had managed to gain Churchill's ear and had persuaded him that he would be better in the post. Ironside was told merely that the Cabinet wanted someone *'with recent combat experience'* in the post. Once again, he was out. Ironside accepted the decision gracefully, saying:

'I had done my best ... I can't complain. Cabinets have to make decisions in times of stress. I don't suppose that Winston liked doing it, for he is always loyal to his friends.'

It was effectively the end of Ironside's military career, although he was promoted to Field Marshal for his service in August 1940 and given a peerage as Baron Ironside of Archangel and of Ironside in the County of Aberdeen. Ironside retired to Morley Old Hall in Norfolk and took no further part in the war. He divided his time between writing and farming.

Throughout his career, Ironside had kept a daily diary which was raw, outspoken and which he never intended for publication. However – like some brother officers – he was alarmed to see certain accounts of the war which were somewhat slanted starting to be published and accepted as fact. Given this, he finally gave his permission to publish a selection of his diary entries from 1937-1940 in 1958. Full publication followed five years later

Ironside died in September 1959 following a fall at his home and full military honours were accorded him at his funeral in Westminster Abbey.

'My trouble is that I am not really interested in war.'
Wavell

'..a good average Colonel...(who) would make a good chairman of a Tory association.'
Winston Churchill

'(The only British General) who showed a touch of genius was Wavell.'
Field Marshal Rommel

'Winston is always expecting rabbits to come out of empty hats.''
Wavell

WAVELL - THE SCHOLAR

Archibald Wavell was too gifted and too clever for the army. That was essentially what his headmaster at Winchester College, Dr. Fearon, told Wavell's father when the two men met to discuss his son's future. Perturbed to learn that Wavell was destined for Sandhurst Military Academy, Dr. Fearon argued that the young Wavell had *'sufficient ability to make his way in other walks of life'* and there therefore was no need for him to go into the army at all. Nevertheless, the army would be his destiny.

A devout Christian and lover of poetry, Wavell possessed a fierce intelligence that allowed him to finish the Times crossword puzzle each morning in less than twenty minutes. However, what he did not possess, it was said, was the *'killer instinct'* necessary in the best Commanders. That was certainly what Churchill thought. His men thought better of him. To them he was *'The Chief'*

Archibald Percival Wavell was born into a military family in Colchester on May 5th 1883. An undeniably bright little boy, his parents delighted in showing him off to guests and it left Wavell with a lifelong shyness he could never quite conquer.

On graduating from Sandhurst (at the top of his class), Wavell was commissioned into the infantry, joining the Black Watch, part of the Royal Regiment of Scotland which had a long history of distinguished actions on the African Continent. Wavell experienced his first taste of action in the Second Boer War, before being transferred to India in 1903. Now nicknamed 'Podgy' by his brother officers, he was promoted to Lieutenant in 1904 and fought in the Bazar Valley Campaign of 1908 under General Sir James Willcocks, helping to quell unruly Pathan tribesmen in the Peshawar border area of India's North West Frontier (now Pakistan).

Wavell's academic abilities were still getting noticed and, in January 1909 he was seconded to attend the Army Staff College back home in Camberley. Naturally, Wavell finished his studies with an A Grade. Wavell was a Captain serving as a Staff Officer when the Great War began. He quickly found himself posted to the continent to serve at the British Expeditionary Force's general HQ. In November 1914, as the British Army reeled from its early losses, he was swiftly appointed Brigade Major of the 9th Infantry Brigade. On April 22nd 1915, Wavell married Eugenie Marie Quirk. They would have three daughters and a son. On returning from honeymoon to the front, he was caught up in the Second Battle of Ypres in Belgium, losing his left eye in action to a shell splinter and receiving a Military Cross for his gallantry. After convalescing, Wavell first returned to the British General HQ in France before serving as a liaison officer to Russian forces fighting in the Caucasus Mountains and then with the Egyptian Expeditionary Force where he met General Sir Edmund Allenby – a man who was to have a great

influence on him. From there he served with the Supreme War Council in Versailles before shipping out again to Palestine in March 1918. By war's end, he had risen in the ranks to Brigadier General.

Despite the carnage that was the First World War, there were just too many officers on the books for the British Army's needs once the shooting had stopped. More than once, Wavell had to accept a demotion to get a posting and spent significant amounts of time effectively unemployed and on half pay. Sometimes life would be hard and Wavell would have to supplement his income by writing entries for the Encyclopaedia Britannica or giving lectures. In better times, Wavell would enjoy plum positions, including assistant Adjutant General at the War Office and aide-de-camp to King George VI himself. By 1937 Wavell found himself back in the Middle East as General Officer commanding British Forces in Palestine and Trans-Jordan. The following year he was promoted to Lieutenant General and became General Officer Commanding-in-Chief Southern Command in Britain. As war threatened in 1939, he was promoted to General and in July 1939, appointed General Officer Commanding-in-Chief of Middle East Command.

When war broke out in September 1939, events remained calm in the Middle East for a good nine months and Wavell was essentially side-lined from any action. It was only when Italy joined the war in June 1940 on the side of the Germans that things finally flared up. The Italians had significant colonial interests in North and East Africa and a full scale clash was inevitable. The British found themselves at a significant and immediate disadvantage in terms of both men and materials. Implementing a tactic of 'flexible containment', Wavell withdrew as Italian forces came bursting out of Libya to his West and Eritrea and Ethiopia to his South.

On August 7th 1940 Wavell flew back to London. He clashed with Churchill over supplies and men. He wanted more. Churchill had little to give and – in the dark days of the summer of 1940 when the invasion of Britain seemed imminent – Churchill was reduced to dolling out fine oratory instead of men and materials. Wavell knew fine oratory and knew it wouldn't fill the petrol tanks of his armour or the magazines of his fighting men. He did not try to match Churchill's eloquence but met his verbal assaults with a stony silence or truculent one word responses. This only infuriated Churchill more – and frightened him. It reminded him of how General Haig had behaved before Lloyd George during the Great War – and the last thing Churchill wanted was another Haig. Wavell came away convinced that Churchill's sense of tactics had been formed during the Boer War and that the Prime Minister didn't know what to make of him. However, he also came away – much to his utter amazement - with a precious convoy of tanks, artillery pieces and ammunition for his theatre of war.

During August, the Italians caused some minor mischief in British Somaliland in which Allied forces acquitted themselves rather well. However, Mussolini filled the air waves with boasts of one great fictitious victory after another – and Churchill believed him. Churchill was furious and started referring to some Generals in Africa who deserved to be shot. The low casualty figures the British had sustained (less than 250 compared to over 2,000 Italian dead and wounded) were interpreted as a sign that the British forces had been cowardly. He blazed off a furious cable to Wavell, who – equally furious - replied *'A big butcher's bill is not necessarily evidence of good tactics!'* When he received the reply, Churchill was said to be struck almost dumb with anger. General Dill said he had never seen the Prime Minister so angry. Wavell was now living on borrowed time – but Churchill had no idea who to replace him with.

When he had amassed sufficient forces, Wavell struck back. He had kept his plans secret from Churchill because he didn't trust the security of communications and had instead only told Anthony Eden about them when he visited Egypt in person. Eden dutifully reported Wavell's plans to Churchill who apparently now *'purred like six cats'.*

In December 1940, Wavell masterminded Operation Compass, an assault on Libya from Egypt across the Western Desert. It was a stunning military success. By February 1941, the Italian 10th Army was all but broken and reeling in shock, having lost hundreds of tanks and over a thousand artillery pieces and warplanes. Wavell had advanced 500 miles in just ten weeks. 130,000 Italian soldiers had been scooped up and taken prisoner. Allied losses were just 555 men killed and a further 1,373 wounded. Wavell's forces seemed on the brink of a stunning victory. Libya was open to them, theirs for the taking. And then the advance was stopped dead.

Churchill, gravely concerned for the fate of Greece and the Aegean and bounded by security assurances given to the Greek nation, had ordered Wavell to divert essential troops and supplies to Greece to defend it from Axis forces. Wavell complained, pleading to be allowed

CIRCA 1936: General Archibald Percival Wavell during a visit to Charterhouse School

CLOCKWISE FROM TOP LEFT: APRIL 1941: Generals Wavell and Quinan (left) in the Middle East; MAY 1943: Aboard the SS Queen Mary, around a conference table sit Wavell with Winston Churchill and Admiral Sir James Somerville; 17TH JUNE 1946: Wavell, Montgomery and Auchinleck discuss their progress; 5TH JANUARY 1942: Wavell inspects a trench mortar section of a Dogra regiment during his visit to Singapore to finish the job in Libya, but Churchill was in no mood to listen. Wavell, in a sudden about turn that surprised even Churchill, suddenly agreed to the diversion of precious resources to Greece. The campaign failed and valuable men and equipment were quickly swallowed by the conflagration. As pressure eased up on the remaining beleaguered Italian units in Libya, they were reinforced by much stronger and more skilled and determined troops - the German Afrika Korps under Rommel. In just two months, the Afrika Korps hurled the British all the way back into Egypt again, laid siege to the garrison at Tobruk (which would not be relieved for 240 days) and effectively undid everything Wavell had achieved. In his tent, Rommel had been reading Wavell's influential book Generals and Generalship – and had learned much about his opponent from it. At home, Churchill grumbled:

'Wavell ... has been very silly in North Africa and should have been prepared to meet an attack there.'

Wavell again found himself in Churchill's bad books when he fought against sending part of his precious remaining forces to free Iraq from Pro-Axis forces. Now Wavell struggled. Spurred on by Churchill to get faster results, his assaults on the Vichy forces in Syria and Lebanon met stiffer resistance than expected and Operation Battleaxe – Wavell's attempt to relieve the besieged British garrison at Tobruk - failed in mid-June. The new German .88 anti-tank guns tore British armour to pieces before they could even close with Rommel's panzers. Fifty per cent were knocked out in the first day of action.

On June 22nd, Churchill told Wavell that General Auchinleck would be replacing him. Wavell was philosophical when he received the news. *'The Prime Minister's quite right. This job needs a new eye and a new hand,'* he said.

Wavell was given Auchinleck's previous job as Commander-in-Chief, India Command. Although the area it covered was absolutely vast, it was much quieter and Churchill most probably thought that Wavell could be safely side-lined there to be efficient but unexciting. *'Wavell will enjoy sitting under a pagoda tree,'* he chuckled. Churchill had forgotten one thing – The Japanese. On December 8th 1941, the Japanese launched attacks on Singapore, Malaya and Hong Kong, leading Britain to declare war on them.

Now Wavell found himself in the hottest new theatre of the war. By the spring of 1942, the Japanese had swept westward as far as Burma and there was no prospect of saving even that. Wavell ordered all British and Commonwealth forces in the country to withdraw to India and reconsolidate. There was a good danger that even India itself might fall. Wavell did try to counter-attack in September 1942 but met stiff and determined Japanese resistance and had to withdraw to India once more by March 1943.

Effectively, the failure of the assault on Burma ended Wavell's military career, although he was promoted to Field Marshal in January 1943. He was replaced once more by Auchinleck and given the job of Viceroy of India. In keeping with his grand new role, Wavell was made Viscount Wavell of Cyrenaica and of Winchester. Perhaps by now rather philosophical about where his life was going, Wavell took advantage of his spare time to compile a bestselling anthology of poetry, Other Men's Flowers (1944). All those pieces in the book he knew by heart. He even contributed one of his own poems to the collection, describing it as a *'... little wayside dandelion of my own'.*

However, by sheer bad luck, Wavell now found himself in another position that was about to explode. India was coming apart, riven with violence and ethnic hatreds between Moslems and Hindus and racked by waves of nationalist anti-colonial fervour. Wavell was simply not cunning or duplicitous enough for the job. He tried to play fair with everybody – which warmed him to nobody. He tried to warn both Churchill and his successor as Prime Minister Clement Attlee of the desperate situation developing on the Indian sub-continent. Neither wanted to know. India was Wavell's problem – at least until Attlee lost patience with him and abruptly replaced him at one month's notice with Lord Mountbatten in 1947. 'Not very courteously done, ' was Wavell's assessment of his dismissal.

Wavell returned to Britain in 1947, to the much less grand post of High Steward of Colchester. He briefly became associated with a number of prestigious literary societies - but ill-heath prevented him from becoming more fully immersed in the true love of his life. He died on May 24th 1950 of complications following earlier abdominal surgery. On 7th June, his funeral procession set off along the Thames from the Tower of London where his body had been lying in state en route to Westminster Abbey. Prime Minister Attlee was there to say his farewells, as were Lord Halifax and Field Marshals Alanbrooke and Montgomery. Winston Churchill did not attend. Wavell is buried in the grounds of his old college at Winchester.

'Of General Auchinleck I will only say that he is an Officer of the greatest distinction, and of a character of singular elevation'
Winston Churchill

'Auchinleck, to my mind, had most of the qualifications to make him one of the finest of Commanders, but unfortunately he lacked the most important of all – the ability to select the men to serve him.'
General Brooke

AUCHINLECK - MAN OF EMPIRE

They called him 'The Auk' or 'The Auk of India'. Claude John Eyre Auchinleck was born in the garrison town of Aldershot on June 21st 1884. His father, a Colonel in the Royal Artillery, died when his son was eight and the family was financially distressed. A good education was only possible because Auchinleck won scholarships to first Eagle House School and then Wellington College. where he won the Derby Gift - a prize of £50 awarded for industry and good conduct which changed his young life – and which allowed him to go on to attend Sandhurst Military College.

Upon leaving Sandhurst with only middling marks, Auchinleck was posted to India as a Second Lieutenant in 1903 and, a year later, joined the infantry as part of the 62nd Punjabis. He had wanted to join the Royal Artillery like his father, but could not muster the mathematics. However, his willingness to learn and speak Punjabi made him popular with the men under his command. By 1912, he was a Captain.

During the First World War, Auchinleck moved with his regiment when they were posted to Egypt to defend the Suez Canal against Turkish Ottoman forces. He fought against the Turks at Ismailia in February 1915 before being posted to Aden in July that year to counter a further Turkish threat. By December 1915, his regiment was in Mesopotamia. In January 1916, he fought in the disastrous Battle of Hanna, which saw an Allied relief column fighting its way up the Tigris River to join Anglo-Indian forces some 10,000 strong trapped by the Turks at the town of Kut-al-Amara. On January 21st 1916, the relief force of 10,000 men slammed up against heavily fortified Turkish trenches containing some 30,000 soldiers. Under heavy machine gun fire, the Allied troops tried to storm the Turkish lines across 600 yards of flooded and treacherous no-man's land. It was a massacre. Over 2,700 men were killed or wounded and what remained of the relief column had to hurriedly retreat to safety. Auchinleck was one of the few officers to survive. The experience vividly brought home to the young Auchinleck the problem with attacking well-fortified defensive positions bristling with machine guns and instilled in him a real sense of caution that was to temper his aggressive instincts on the battlefield.

By July 1916, Auchinleck was acting Major and second in command of his regiment. In February 1917, he became acting Commander of the 62nd Punjabis and led them through the Second Battle of Kut through to the taking of Baghdad. His actions earned him a D.S.O. and a mention in dispatches and, by 1919, he was promoted to Brevet Lieutenant-Colonel.

The war over, Auchinleck returned to India to study at the Staff College in Quetta from 1920 to 1921. While on leave from India, playing tennis on the French Riviera, he met his future wife 21-year-old Jessie Stewart from America. Auchinleck was 37 and completely smitten. Within five months they were married. Jessie returned with him to India, where she settled in well and became known as 'that little American girl'.

CIRCA 1914: 62nd Punjabis, now 1 Punjab, Pakistan Army, Ismailia, Egypt, 1914. Captain Claude Auchinleck is standing on far right

CIRCA 1941: Auchinleck, Commander-in-Chief, in the Middle East

By 1930, Auchinleck was a Colonel and teaching at the Staff College in Quetta. After three years' service, he was further promoted to acting Brigadier and given command of the Peshawar Brigade to help crush rebellious tribes. He took part in both the Mohmand and Bajaur campaigns, and returned in 1935 to lead the Second Mohmand Campaign in August 1935 alongside Alexander. At the end of 1935, he was promoted to Major-General. After a period of 'unemployment' on half pay, Auchinleck became deputy chief of the General Staff and director of staff duties in Delhi in September 1936 and assumed command of India's Meerut District in 1938. That same year, he chaired a committee looking into almost every aspect of the Indian Army.

Auchinleck was abruptly recalled from India to command IV Corps in January 1940. Now a Lieutenant General, he was given command of the Anglo-French forces fighting in Norway in May 1940, Auchinleck demanded more supplies, artillery and air support from Churchill. He didn't get any of it and the operation proved a disaster. Churchill, typically, blamed it on Auchinleck for being too conservative and not daring enough.

A month later he was back in Britain and in charge of V Corps before rapidly moving on to become General Officer Commanding-in-Chief, Southern Command, where he had a particularly testy relationship with his subordinate, one Bernard Montgomery. ' I cannot recall that we ever agreed on anything,' Montgomery said later. Auchinleck seriously considered dismissing Montgomery for what he considered to be his deliberate insubordination, but stopped himself. With a German invasion seeming imminent, there were more important things to do.

On Boxing Day, 1940, Auchinleck was promoted to full General. A month later he was sent back to his beloved India as Commander-in-Chief. While he had upset Churchill by telling journalists that what was needed to win the war was American troops, he did regain Churchill's favour in April 1941, by rapidly despatching Allied forces west by air and sea to RAF Habbaniya when it was threatened by pro-Nazi Iraqi forces. Churchill had encountered extreme reluctance from his Commander-in-Chief Middle East Command , General Wavell, to spare troops. And Churchill kept score. By July, Wavell and Auchinleck had swapped places. Auchinleck was now Commander-in-Chief Middle East Command and Wavell was Commander-in-Chief, India – a much less active command.

At first, it looked as though Auchinleck was the man for the job.. In November 1941, he launched Operation Crusader much to Churchill's approval. *'For the first time, the Germans are getting a taste of their own bitter medicine,'* he exalted. By December, Crusader had relieved the besieged garrison at Tobruk. However, Auchinleck became too confident, describing the Axis forces as *'hard pressed'* on January 12th 1942. Just a few days later, Rommel launched a ferocious counter attack that sent British and Dominion forces into full retreat. Brooke saw

4 NOVEMBER 1941: Auchinleck, decorating Lieutenant Colonel Howard Karl Kippenberger with the Distinguished Service Order in the Western Desert

5TH AUGUST 1942: Western desert, Egypt. Auchinleck (RIGHT) with Churchill, Lieutenant-General Sir Leslie Morshead and Lieutenant-General Ramsden

1ST OCTOBER 1945: Auchinleck receives the Most Refulgent Order of the Star of Nepal, First Class, from the King of Nepal

this as *'nothing less than bad generalship on the part of Auchinleck'.*

By May 1942, Tobruk had fallen to the Axis powers. 25,000 Allied POWs were taken at Tobruk and the British Army had been forced well back. Taking control of the 8th Army – the 'Desert Rats' – away from his subordinate, General Ritchie, Auchinleck managed to at least halt the German advance at the First Battle of El Alamein on July 1st, but despite a number of counter-attacks could not hurl them back westwards once again.

A stalemate ensued. It became increasingly clear that Auchinleck had lost the confidence of both his subordinate officers and senior Dominion Commanders. He had also lost the confidence of Churchill and Brooke, who flew out to Cairo in August 1942 and replaced him with General Alexander. Churchill later recalled the sacking thus: *'It was',* he said, *'like shooting a magnificent stag'.*

In a face-saving gesture, Churchill offered Auchinleck a post as head of a proposed Persia and Iraq Command but Auchinleck turned it down. Instead, he returned to India where he spent a year virtually unemployed before being appointed Commander-in-Chief, India once more, working alongside General Wavell who was now the Viceroy. General Slim later praised Auchinleck's work behind the scenes in ensuring that his 'forgotten army' was not entirely forgotten when fighting in Burma:

In November 1943, the newly created South East Asia Command under Admiral Louis Mountbatten took responsibility for the war against the Japanese in the East, relegating Auchinleck's remit to the defence of India and its functions as a military base.

In 1944, Auchinleck was shattered when it was discovered that his wife Jessie was having an affair with Air Chief Marshal Sir Richard Peirse. Auchinleck finally divorced her in 1946, but the damage was done. A family member describes him as never being the same after the collapse of his marriage and – for the rest of his life – Auchinleck would still carry his wife's picture in his wallet.

In 1946, Auchinleck was promoted to Field Marshal as he struggled with the forthcoming Independence for India and the threat of Partition, which he saw as disastrous. Still, he did his best to help break the existing army into separate Indian and Pakistani units. It was a terrible thing to have to do – to help preside over the breakup of a country he so loved. Auchinleck turned down a peerage over the issue and argued desperately for the use of British troops to help keep the peace and save lives during the transformation. Mountbatten disagreed and overruled him. No one knows how many people were killed during Partition. Some estimates say up to four million. After Partition, in August 1947, he became Supreme Commander of all British forces left in both India and Pakistan and stayed on until the Supreme HQ was closed in November 1948. Then he came home.

Auchinleck spent his remaining days alternating between business and charitable activities. In his spare time, he liked to paint watercolours. In 1968, tired of the British climate, he emigrated to Marrakesh in Morocco, He died there on 23rd March 1981 aged 96 and is today buried in a Commonwealth war cemetery in Casablanca.

◀ 19TH AUGUST 1942: Auchinleck with Churchill and other high ranking officers in gardens of the British Embassy, the Middle East

'It is undeniable that Colonel Alexander had the gift of handling the men on the lines to which they most readily responded ... His subordinates loved him, even when he fell upon them blisteringly for their shortcomings; and his men were all his own.'
Rudyard Kipling

'He likes to talk of other things – politics, ancient art (especially Roman antiquities), country life. He hates war.'
Harold Macmillan

ALEXANDER – THE DANDY

Harold Rupert Leofric George Alexander reached some impressive heights in his career. Not only did he attain the rank of Field Marshal the Right Honourable the Earl Alexander of Tunis but he also became Chief Eagle Head of the Blackfoot Indians.

Those who knew him said that Alexander had movie star looks. Moreover, he looked exactly how a British General should look up on the Big Screen – handsome, aristocratic and possessed of a small but dashing waxed moustache. He was physically brave and even reckless in the face of danger. The Americans were, of course, smitten with him and even a little in awe.

Alexander was born into privilege in London on December 10th 1891, the third son of the Earl and Countess of Caledon. His parents called him 'Baby'. Alexander's father died when he was six and his mother Elizabeth proved aloof and distant. As a consequence the young Alexander spent much of his childhood until the age of ten happily running wild on the family's Irish estate, riding ponies, shooting, canoeing and playing war games with his brothers. When indoors, he learned to play the side drums.

Educated at Harrow, Alexander proved an exceptional sportsman in everything he tried from boxing to gymnastics, but he was a mediocre student at best. He toyed with the idea of becoming an artist before settling for a military career and entering Sandhurst Military College in 1910. From Sandhurst, he received his first commission as a Second Lieutenant with the Irish Guards.

Alexander still dreamed of being an artist and planned to leave the army after a few years' service. The Great War changed everything. He was despatched to France with the British Expeditionary Force shortly after war was declared in 1914. He was now 22 years old and a Platoon Commander with 1st Battalion, The Irish Guards. His unit took part in the first major British action of the war, the Battle of Mons, and he was part of the British retreat when the French flank crumbled, a retreat that ended with the desperate stopping action to save Paris that was the First Battle of the Marne. Later in 1914, during the First Battle of Ypres, he was wounded in in the thigh and the hand and shipped home. Returning to the Western Front, he fought at Loos in 1915, receiving a Military Cross for his actions. The following year, he was awarded the D.S.O. during the Somme offensive. His citation read:

'For conspicuous gallantry in action. He was the life and soul of the attack, and throughout the day led forward not only his own men but men of all regiments. He held the trenches gained in spite of heavy machine gun fire.'

Alexander continued to fight with the Guards for much for the remainder of the war, including further actions at the Somme, Passchendaele and Cambrai and was wounded again at the Third Battle of Ypres. He was

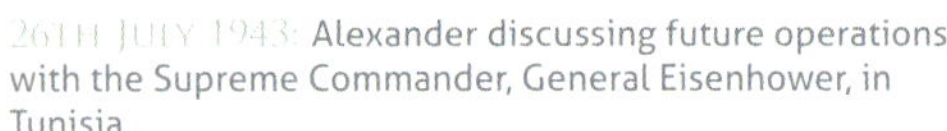
26TH JULY 1943: Alexander discussing future operations with the Supreme Commander, General Eisenhower, in Tunisia

CIRCA 1944: Portrait of Alexander, in his headquarters, Royal Palace, Caserta, Italy

CICA 1944: Alexander and aide at his desk, at his headquarters, Royal Palace, Caserta, Italy

now an acting Lieutenant Colonel and it has been said that he personally led his men 'over the top' on 30 offensives during the course of the war. He later described those war years as *'the happiest years of my life.'* He had continued to paint while in the trenches, but had come to realise that the military was his calling after all. Those he had fought beside were full of praise for his courage – and for the way he had happily forsaken many of the privileges fellow officers enjoyed to better share the conditions of his men.

In 1919, Alexander joined the Baltische Landeswehr, commanding an odd mix of German regular soldiers and Latvian territorials as they fought to stop the Russian Bolsheviks occupying the Baltic. The early 1920s saw Alexander almost constantly on the move. Between home postings, he was in Constantinople (where in his spare time he taught Turkish officers how to do an Irish jig), then Gibraltar. 1930 saw Alexander sent to the Imperial Defence College for a year. Here he was tutored by both Alan Brooke and Bernard Montgomery. Neither of them thought particularly highly of him and Montgomery later wrote *'(we) came to the conclusion then that he had no brains – and we were right'.* In October 1931, after completing his studies, Alexander married Lady Margaret Bingham. The couple were to have three children, and later to adopt a fourth.

After a series of staff appointments in Britain, Alexander was made a temporary Brigadier and sent to the North West Frontier of India to command the Nowshera Brigade. He soon became popular with his men thanks to his willingness to learn Urdu. The following year he was made a Companion of the Order of the Star of India for his gallant actions in Malakand against the rebellious Pathan tribesmen and was also mentioned in despatches. Later in 1936, he took part in the Second Mohmand Campaign against Marauding Pashtun tribesmen under then Brigadier Claude Auchinleck and insisted in always leading from the front. The following year, he was also promoted to Major General and found himself the youngest General in the British Army at the age of 45.

As war with Germany became increasingly likely, he returned to Britain in 1938 to take command on the 1st Infantry Division. Alexander's division was posted to France as part of I Corps of the British Expeditionary Force and, after the German Blitzkrieg of May 1940, Alexander helped to ensure the successful evacuation of troops at Dunkirk. He cheered up the troops thronging the Dunkirk beaches by building sandcastles in his finest dress uniform as the Stuka dive bombers did their worst. He departed on the very last destroyer after personally traversing the beaches in a small boat shouting, *'Is there anyone there?'* in both French and English to assure that everyone who was to be evacuated had got away.

Now, with Britain under imminent threat of invasion, Alexander was given responsibility for protecting the coastlines of Yorkshire and Lincolnshire. He was promoted to acting Lieutenant General in July 1940 and became General Officer Commanding-in-Chief of Southern Command, where his role was now to defend south-west England.

4th March 1944: Alexander, with US General Truscott, in charge of the Allied bridgehead at Anzio

26TH AUGUST 1944: Alexander discussing the situation in Italy with Churchill and General Sir Oliver Leese at Leese's headquarters in the Monte Maggio area

26TH AUGUST 1944: Auchinleck takes time to pose for a picture with Churchill and General Leese

A month after he was knighted in January 1942, Alexander was appointed GOC-in-C of British Forces in Burma. His orders were to hold Rangoon at all costs but it proved impossible – and Churchill understood that saying, 'never have I taken the responsibility for sending a General on a more forlorn hope'. The Japanese overran it in a matter of weeks and Alexander himself barely evaded capture and indeed death, due to his habit of liking to be close to the front lines. He now commanded a fighting retreat from Burma back to India. Those in high places were very impressed that Alexander got on to very good terms with both Chinese leader Chiang Kai-shek and the American General Joe W. Stilwell during his time in theatre. Both were normally notorious for being difficult and prickly to the point of being impossible to deal with, but Alexander charmed them both.

Alexander was pulled out of the Far East in summer of 1942. Initially he was to be British task force Commander for Operation Torch, but within just a few weeks he was sent to Cairo to replace General Auchinleck as the Commander-in-Chief of Middle East Command at Brooke's suggestion. At the same time, Montgomery assumed control of the 8th Army. Although answerable to Alexander, Montgomery didn't like the man and decided he was going to do essentially as he thought was best and to hell with what his Commanding Officer thought. Although such insubordination would have been disastrous in some commands, this worked because Alexander was casual in his approach to rank as well as very good at delegating to his Commanders, as he had proved with Slim in Burma. Here was a man who liked to *'suggest'* rather than order. This was probably the reason that Montgomery later said of Alexander:

' (He was the) only man under whom any General would gladly serve in a subordinate position'.

In fact, it sometimes felt that Alexander's real role in life was to shield Montgomery from an ever-more impatient Churchill, as his subordinate meticulously made plans for his offensive. The Battle of El Alamein followed in November 1942, and then a British sweep westward to meet in Tunisia with another Anglo-American force 1,600 miles in just eighty days.

The Americans coming in from the west were dazzled by Alexander's natural English charm and Alexander for his part also quickly took to General Eisenhower, commenting: 'Eisenhower is such a nice chap and could not be more frank, friendly and helpful'. In private however, Alexander was shocked at the performance of American soldiers in combat, believing that they were slow in attack, defensively minded and very bomb and shell-shy – as well; as poorly trained and 'soft'. Despite Alexander's severe and sincere misgivings, the North African campaign did end in victory for the Allies. The final Axis surrender in North Africa came on 13th May 1943 and Alexander was able to report to Churchill:

'Sir. It is my duty to report that the Tunisian Campaign is over. All enemy resistance has ceased. We are masters of the North African shores.'

Alexander and Churchill with other officers in North Africa

CIRCA 1944: Alexander with Eisenhower and Churchill, clad in a dressing gown while recovering from an illness, meet somewhere in the Mediterranean

British and American forces now combined as 18th Army Group and Alexander was given command, reporting up to Eisenhower, the Supreme Allied Commander in the Mediterranean. General Bradley was now to praise Alexander for the way he helped develop the American field command – a process surprisingly with little friction – and to describe him as *'a restrained, self-effacive, and punctilious soldier.'* The18th became the 15th Army group and then launched the invasion of the island of Sicily, a hugely successful operation that took just five weeks to complete. However it revealed real problems in the Allied command structure. American and British Commanders alike were found to be tentative when ordering the troops of another nation around, and it was a problem that would continue to blight the whole Italian Campaign. Alexander though was undoubtedly one of the British Commanders who got on best with his American counterparts and who helped to smooth over many potential divisions and spats as the Allies climbed their way up Italy.

Alexander stayed then as Commander of the 15th Army Group until it became the Allied Armies in Italy. In December 1944, General Mark Clark assumed the post and Alexander – now promoted to Field Marshal – personally accepted the German surrender in Italy, on April 29th 1945.

As recognition of his services during the Second World War, Alexander was elevated to the peerage on March 1st 1946 as Viscount Alexander of Tunis and Errigal in the County of Donegal. That same year, Alexander was appointed Viceroy to Canada, a post he held for five years. It was a post he loved and he proved very popular with the Canadian people. He became Chief Scout of Canada and also the first white chief of the Kwakiutl tribe, for which he was given his own totem pole. He would also later become Chief Eagle Head of the Blackfoot People.

Alexander would probably have much preferred to stay Viceroy of Canada for the rest of his days, but duty pulled him back to Britain in 1952. Churchill had personally invited him home to become Minister of Defence in his cabinet. 'I simply can't refuse Winston',' Alexander confessed. Now ailing, Churchill could not continue to hold both the post of Prime Minister and Minister of Defence and had reluctantly agreed to let go of the post. Of course, when the time came, he couldn't do it – and Alexander found Churchill interfering in every aspect of his new job on a fairly incessant basis. Two years later he resigned and never again held political office.

Alexander spent much of his twilight years travelling between Britain and his beloved Canada, visiting family and friends .While at home he gardened, painted and devoted time to his business interests. He died on June 16th 1969 after a sudden heart attack and is today buried in a village churchyard close to his family's Hertfordshire estate. His headstone bears just one word – Alex.

1945: Field Marshal Sir Harold Alexander standing in front of a large map

'..the dead hand of inanition..'
Winston Churchill

'Perhaps the most valuable and best remembered gain was the association with and the friendship of Sir John Dill, whose character, modesty and power of imparting knowledge left a lasting impression on me and, I think, on many others'
General Auchinleck

DILL - THE BRIDGE-BUILDER

His name was General Sir John Greer Dill but, behind his back, Churchill called him 'Dilly-Dally'. It didn't auger well for their relationship.

Unusually for generals in the British Army at the time, Dill didn't originate from a family steeped in military tradition. Born on Christmas Day, 1881 in County Armagh, Ireland, Dill's father was the local bank manager. He was orphaned at the age of 12 and he and his sister were taken in by an uncle and aunt. By all accounts his childhood was lonely. He lacked the ability to make friends easily and – almost to the end of his life – that would remain a problem. After schooling at the Methodist College, Belfast he attended Cheltenham College, where his science teacher commented that he was one of the slowest pupils he had ever tried to teach. Dill then attended Sandhurst Military Academy and graduated 154th out of 210 to join the infantry - the 1st Battalion the Prince of Wales's Leinster Regiment. He had been a mediocre student at best, but his good manners and behaviour were frequently praised. His first active service posting was to South Africa during the Second Boer War, where he took part in small operations in Cape Colony, the Orange River Colony and the Transvaal.

In 1907, he married Ada Le Motte. Their only child, John, was born in 1916. After her death in 1940, Dill would marry again in October 1941. This time his bride was Nancy Charrington – a much younger woman.

When the First World War broke out, Dill was promoted to Brigade-Major and despatched to France with the 25th Brigade. Over the course of the war, he was mentioned in despatches no less than eight times and won promotion to temporary Brigadier. Dill was a Major General by 1930 and served at the War Office as Director of Military Operations and Intelligence until 1936. In September that year, he was appointed General Officer commanding British Forces in Palestine, holding the post until 1937 – the year he received his knighthood - but returned the following year to serve as General Officer commanding Aldershot Command. When war broke out, Dill was assigned command of 1st Army Corps in France and promoted to full General a month later. He returned to Britain in April 1940 to take up the role of Vice Chief of the Imperial General Staff. He came back to a world in chaos because of the Norwegian campaign, and wrote back to General Gort who was still in the field;

'The War Office is, as far as I can see, in complete chaos and the situation in Norway as bad as I expected...I'm not sure Winston isn't the greatest menace. No-one seems able to control him. He is full of ideas, many brilliant, but most of them impractical'.

On May 25th, Churchill fired the-then CIGS General Ironside and promoted Dill in his place. He was fifty-nine years old. Churchill soon realised that Dill's appointment to CIGS was a bad mistake. As early as July 1940, he confessed:

DECEMBER 1940: Dill converses with glider pilots and inspects a training glider at the Central Landing Establishment at RAF Ringway near Manchester

CIRCA 1941:Conference leaders during Church services on the deck of HMS Prince of Wales, Placentia Bay, Newfoundland, Dill stands behind Churchill

' I do not think we are having the help from General Dill which we hoped for at the time of his appointment, and he strikes me as being very tired, disheartened and over-impressed by the might of Germany.'

Few allowances were made for Dill's personal circumstances, with his wife Ada slowly dying of progressive strokes. (She finally succumbed in December 1940.) Only General Brooke – himself a widower - seemed to understand what hell Dill was living through, writing:

'Every visit home to his wife in Windsor was a desperate ordeal; she could not make herself understood, he kept guessing at what she could mean, usually unsuccessfully, and finally with a disappointed look in her eyes she used to throw her head back on the pillow'

However, it was not just his personal circumstances that were weighing on him. The role of CIGS was also almost beyond him, with Churchill making constant and sometimes bizarre impositions on him. He complained:

'I live a very hectic life. Most of it is spent trying to prevent stupid things being done rather than in doing clever things!'

Churchill and Dill fought. Dill was cautious, Churchill always looking for the next method and means of attack. Trying to avoid such ferocious clashes, Dill would often resort to sending Churchill detailed, carefully crafted explanatory notes and memos. This was not how to do business with Winston Churchill.

For his part, Churchill found Dill slow, unimaginative and even an obstruction to the war effort. He was considered to be exhausted if not physically ill. In the parlance of the day he was *'a tired man'*. He was *'Dilly-Dally'*. Churchill was not his only detractor. Lord Moran said archly that Dill *'lacked the he-man stuff'*. Others were frankly astounded at his choices of officer appointees and a number of his strategic decisions. Dill hated the Russians and saw any attempts to support them as weakening Britain's own resources and such depletion might also weaken Britain in the Pacific, where war against the Japanese was now ever more likely. He did not share Churchill's enthusiasm for supporting them when they entered the war in July 1941. Furthermore, worn down and exhausted, Dill genuinely was despondent after the failure of the Greek campaign, which he had advised against but had been overruled. He was similarly shaken by the Afrika Korps victories in Libya in April 1941. *'I think it is desperate,'* he confessed. *'I am terribly tired'*. He considered resignation. Later, he confided to a fellow senior officer, *'I suppose you realise that we shall lose the Middle East.'*

Churchill could tolerate almost anything except defeatism (and whistling). The Prime Minister desperately wanted to be rid of him but

CIRCA 1941: Dill visits Maadi Camp. From left: Brigadiers R Miles and E Puttick, Generals Freyberg and Dill, Brigadiers J Hargest and H E Barrowclough

CIRCA 1941: Dill and Churchill (nearest tank) in the turrets of 2 Churchill I tanks during a demonstration of the new vehicle at Vauxhall's at Luton

could not think of anyone any better to promote to CIGS. Almost reluctantly, he chose General Brooke and finally fired Dill in the closing days of 1941. It was a decision understood by most of the military command. As General Ismay wrote:

'The one thing that was necessary and indeed that Winston preferred, was someone to stand up to him, instead of which Jack Dill merely looked, and was bitterly hurt.'

Churchill then had Dill promoted to Field Marshal with the intent of sending him somewhere, anywhere... just as long as it was far away. India was the first choice, but when that didn't happen, on Brooke's suggestion Dill found himself posted to Washington D.C. to act as the Chief of the British joint staff mission and later as senior British representative on the combined Chiefs of Staff. The posting surprised him. In a letter to General Wavell, he said;

'It is odd that Winston should want me to represent him here when he clearly was glad to get me out of the CIGS job. We disagreed too often...'

If Dill's military skills were ever in doubt, his new-found diplomatic skills more than made up for them. Dill set about his task with a rare energy as well as a charm that won over his American colleagues. He became particularly good friends with the U.S. Army Chief of Staff General George C. Marshall. The two had met before Dill's posting to America and got on well. Now they worked together quite splendidly providing advice for President Roosevelt. Their relationship allowed for genuine trust, and the two often showed each other documents that were not, strictly speaking, made to be shared. Marshall recalled

'I had to be very careful that nobody knew this – no one in the U.S. War Department and certainly not the British Chiefs of Staff, because Dill would be destroyed in a minute if this was discovered.'

Dill did not live to see the fruits of his labours. He died on November 4th 1944 of aplastic anaemia, aged 62. His American colleagues mourned him fulsomely. A memorial service was held for Dill in Washington National Cathedral, after which his body was taken through streets lined by thousands of soldiers and finally interred at Arlington National Cemetery. The American Chiefs of Staff were the pallbearers at his funeral. An attendee at the funeral said he had never seen so many sad and shaken faces, and noted that Dill's long time friend General Marshall was 'truly stricken'. Marshall read the lesson at the ceremony.

Dill's statue, in Arlington National Cemetery, depicts him on horseback – one of only two such equestrian statues in the cemetery. There is no statue of Dill in Britain. In the later war years, Brooke had proposed him for a peerage. Churchill refused to back the suggestion.

'An exceptional Officer in every way. I have never met a Commanding Officer who has, to a great extent, the respect and affection of both Officers and men of his battalion'
Lieutenant-General Walter Leslie

'His jumbonic majesty'
Harold Macmillan

WILSON - THE DEPENDABLE

Henry Maitland Wilson weighed 224lb and stood over six feet tall, and so they called him 'Jumbo'. He was popular with both his fellow officers and the men who served under him.

Henry Maitland Wilson was born the son of Army Captain and member of the Suffolk gentry Arthur Wilson in London on September 5th 1881. After schooling at Eton and Sandhurst military academy, he joined the Rifle Brigade as a 2nd Lieutenant in 1900 and saw action during the Second Boer War. His service with the regiment then took him to Egypt and on to India and Ireland.

In 1914, Wilson married Hester Mary Wykeham and they would go on to have one son and one daughter, Patrick and Maud. Wilson was sent to the Western Front in December 1915. He served as a GSO2 on the Somme as part of the New Army's 41st division and the following year served with XIX infantry corps at Passchendaele. In October 1917 he was promoted to temporary Lieutenant Colonel and joined the New Zealand Division. For his war service he was awarded the D.S.O. in 1917 and was mentioned three times in dispatches.

After a series of inter-war postings, the summer of 1939 saw the now Lieutenant General Wilson as General Officer Commanding of British Forces in Egypt and desperately trying to scrape together a half-decent army before war broke out. Convinced that the immediate threat came from Italian colonial forces to the west, he stationed the bulk of what he had in defensive positions at Mersa Matruh, 100 miles inside Egypt from the border with Libya – and waited.

By the start of June 1940, Western Desert Force as it was now designated was still waiting at Mersa Matruh. On June 10th, Italy declared war – and Wilson immediately pounced (within one minute of the declaration) – unleashing his forces on the offensive into Libya. It was a bold move – but unfortunately premature. A week later France collapsed and sued for peace. French forces to the West in Tunisia stopped fighting, freeing up four Italian divisions to turn east and meet Wilson head on. The Italian Commander was reluctant to go on the offensive against Wilson – but then died in a mysterious 'friendly fire' incident which has never been explained. His replacement was perhaps understandably more aggressive.

By September 1940, Italian forces were sweeping east into Egypt itself aiming for control of the Suez Canal - and Wilson found himself badly outnumbered. He had just over 30,000 men facing an invading Italian force of 80,000 – and the Italians could field at least double the number of tanks and artillery pieces too. However, as the Italians came east their supply lines became

CLOCKWISE FROM TOP LEFT: Lieutenant General Sir Henry Maitland Wilson, inspects men of the captured Tripolitanian Camel Corps, Libya.; APRIL 1944: Wilson discusses the battle situation, using a map spread on the bonnet of his car, with Lieutenant General Sir Oliver Leese, at Eighth Army Battle Headquarters in the Mignano area.; 1943: Winston Churchill, recovering from a bout of pneumonia, with General Eisenhower (left), General Sir Henry Maitland-Wilson (right) and other military chiefs, Italy; 1944: Wilson standing in front of a map of Italy in Caserta badly extended and their forces strung out all along the Western Desert. On December 7th, Wilson launched Operation Compass and neatly cut the Italian forces in two. By February 1941, the Italians had suffered bitter losses, including hundreds of tanks, over a thousand big guns and 115,000 men taken prisoner. British forces were now occupying Central Libya – and Churchill was a happy man.

Wilson was rewarded by the post of Military Governor of Cyrenaica (eastern Libya) but by April 1941 was re-posted to Greece with a 62,000 strong Commonwealth Expeditionary Force (W Force) tasked with supporting the Greeks against Nazi aggression.

'...we all send you the order 'Full Steam Ahead!' Churchill wrote to him. It was a disastrous move. Allied forces were greatly outnumbered and communications with their Greek counterparts were poor to non-existent. Enemy aircraft numbered over 1,000. The RAF could barely muster 80. The Greek Army progressively fell apart and their Prime Minister committed suicide. By April 29th, Wilson had completed the unhappy task of evacuating what was left of his forces mainly to Crete (from where they would have to flee from again less than a month later) – and 26 fully-laden troop ships were sunk by the Luftwaffe during the evacuation. In total, Allied forces took 15,000 casualties, as well as losing all their artillery and heavy equipment. There was a lot of blame to go around following the debacle, and Wilson got more than his fair share, but was nevertheless promoted to full General.

From Greece, Wilson was reassigned as General Officer Commanding, British Forces in Palestine and Trans-Jordan and distinguished himself by fighting a successful campaign against French Vichy forces in Syria and the Lebanon, as well as crushing a pro-Nazi rebellion in Iraq. Churchill – still looking upon Wilson with great favour – wanted him to take charge of the Western Desert Force in preparation for an offensive against the newly arrived German Afrika Korps – but met with strong opposition from General Auchinleck, who wanted Lieutenant-General Sir Alan Cunningham in the post instead. Auchinleck got his way and Wilson became instead Commander of the Ninth Army in Syria and Palestine.

Churchill once again championed Wilson in August 1942, suggesting he take over as Commander of the British 8th Army from Auchinleck. Again he was dissuaded, this time by his CIGS General Brooke, who preferred his own protégé Montgomery in the post. Instead, Wilson was given the post of head of the newly created Persia and Iraq Command. He would return to the Western Desert in February 1943, after Montgomery had won his outstanding victory at El Alamein, to take up the post of Commander-in-Chief of the Middle East.

Things were largely quiet in the area for which Wilson was responsible now, but he was imposed upon to launch an attack in the Dodecanese Islands of the Aegean known as Operation Accolade. The Americans were furiously against it but Churchill insisted that it would go ahead regardless, hoping that the move would make Turkey finally enter the war on the Allied side. It didn't. Instead, it resulted in one of the last significant German victories of the war.

Wilson's star was still on the ascendant though. He took over from Eisenhower as the Supreme Allied Commander in the Mediterranean on January 8th 1944, running the Italian Campaign as best he could while more and more men and resources were syphoned away to take part in the Normandy landings and campaign. Following the liberation of Naples in 1944, he is notorious for eating much of the content of the city's aquarium, the Stazione Zoologica.

Wilson held the post for just under a year, before being promoted to Field Marshal and transferred to America as Chief of the British joint staff mission, following the death of General Sir John Dill. Churchill had sent him off with a cable saying, *'I can find only one Officer with the necessary credentials and qualities, namely yourself.'*

Wilson saw out the remainder of the war in Washington and stayed in the post until 1947, by which time he had been created Baron Wilson of Libya and of Stowlangtoft in the County of Suffolk. In 1948, he published his memoirs 'Eight Years Overseas' – and Eisenhower himself provided the introduction. He died on New Year's Eve 1964, in Chilton, Buckinghamshire.

'I don't think in this age in which I have lived, that there has been a man who has been a greater administrator; a man with a knowledge of military affairs equal to General Marshall.'
President Truman

'The only way human beings can win a war is to prevent it.'
General Marshall

'Mr. President, don't call me George.'
General Marshall

MARSHALL - THE PROFESSIONAL

Alastair Cooke once described the wartime head of the American Army as looking like 'a stolid golf-club secretary'. George C. Marshall would have been perfectly happy with that. He was always quiet and modest in company (concealing a foul and volcanic temper), a professional through and through who despised self-promotion and self-aggrandisement. That's probably why he has faded so quickly from history.

George Catlett Marshall Junior was born on New Year's Eve, 1880 in Uniontown, Pennsylvania. His father ran a coal mining business. The youngest of three children, Marshall was a handful as a child and if he and his friends got into trouble, it was certain that it was Marshall who had dreamed up the mischief. His parents were both disappointed by him and worried by his poor performance in school, where the only subject he could distinguish himself in was history.

At the age of 16, Marshall decided to join the Virginia Military Institute. His parents disagreed with his decision, saying he should do 'something more respectable' and his elder brother Stuart begged his mother not to allow Marshall to enrol at the institute as his stupidity would disgrace the family name. The young Marshall overheard them talking, and it straightened him out cold. He did well at the Academy and graduated in 1901, receiving a commission as a Second Lieutenant in the U.S. Army in February 1902. That same year, Marshall married Elizabeth (Lily) Carter Coles. Elizabeth died in 1927. He remarried in 1930, this time to Katherine Boyce Tupper Brown, a widow with three children.

Marshall briefly served in Utah, keeping his eye on a potentially seditious Mormon population before being transferred to The Philippines. He was aide-de-camp to Major General J. Franklin Bell when America declared war on Germany in April 1917, and was heavily involved in mobilising the 1st Division for service in France. He sailed to France on the first troopship and was the second military man ashore. Once overseas, he ended up working closely with the American Commander General John J. 'Blackjack' Pershing. With Pershing, he became instrumental in planning American strategy for the battles of Cantigny, Aisne-Marne, St. Mihiel, and Meuse-Argonne. He emerged from the war with a reputation as a brilliant planner, but never saw action himself.

Between the wars, Marshall held a wide variety of posts as he rose steadily through the ranks. After being assigned to the War Plans Division in Washington D.C. in July 1938, Marshall was appointed Deputy Chief of Staff at the rank of Brigadier General. It was widely believed that he had destroyed his own career when he was the only officer to speak against Roosevelt's plan to build a massive air force. (Marshall said later that he was feeling particularly grumpy on that

CIRCA 1918: Marshall in France during WWI

CIRCA 1943: Marshall with Lieutenant General Walter Krueger and General Douglas MacArthur, at a field headquarters in the Southwest Pacific Area

15TH JULY 1945: Marshall (left) is greeted at the Potsdam Conference

occasion because Roosevelt had called him by his first name and he hated the familiarity.) Marshall wanted to see more resources going to the Army instead, and was suspicious that Roosevelt would give the planes away to other countries – perhaps Britain – when the looming European war finally broke out. Upon leaving the Oval Office, one fellow officer turned to him and said, *'Nice knowing you. Have you ever been to Guam?'*

So it was with some considerable surprise that he was first made acting army Chief of Staff, then promoted to General and confirmed in the post on September 1st 1939 the day Germany invaded Poland. It must have been even more of a shock to the 33 more senior American Generals Roosevelt passed over to give Marshall the job. Roosevelt had, apparently, admired his plain talking. Marshall reminded him – and warned him - of this before accepting the appointment. Their relationship might 'be unpleasant', he cautioned. Roosevelt said merely, 'I know.' Afterwards, their relationship became professionally cordial, but surprisingly detached. Marshall made a point not to socialise with the President and – it is said – even refused to laugh at his jokes. He preferred to communicate with the White House by letters or memos.

When Marshall became Chief of Staff, the strength of the whole U.S. Army stood at just 189,000 men, roughly the same size as the Dutch Army of 1940. Marshall called it *'a little sketchy thing'*. It was also embarrassingly outdated in many aspects. By 1942, he had succeeded in expanding the army fortyfold. Its strength now stood at over eight million men – the largest army in history to that time.

Marshall was undoubtedly over-optimistic and over-eager in pushing for an Allied invasion of mainland Europe in 1942. When the British dissuaded him, convinced that the American Army was not ready, he pushed for 1943 instead. This constant pressure to invade and get at the Germans led General Brooke to say of him:

'In many respects he is a very dangerous man while being a very charming one!'

Churchill fought Marshall vigorously on this, and went over him to President Roosevelt to get a commitment to the invasion of Sicily instead. Marshall knew what the British were doing and was wary of them. He blamed their poor war record to date, the nation's poverty and a fear of receiving heavy casualties for their fear of committing to an invasion.

Having been so involved in the planning, it was always assumed that Marshall would become the Supreme Commander of Operation Overlord. Marshall was expecting it too and already planned to have the British General Dill as his second in command. It was something of a shock when Roosevelt chose Eisenhower instead. *'I didn't feel I could sleep at ease if you were out of Washington,'* he told Marshall. On December 16th 1944,

LEFT TO RIGHT: Marshall, Lieutenant General Frank M. Andrews, Lieutenant General Henry H. Arnold, Major General Oliver P. Echols

CIRCA 1943: Joint Chiefs of Staff lunch. left to right: General Henry H. Arnold, Admiral William D. Leahy, Admiral Ernest J. King and General George C. Marshall

Marshall was promoted to become America's first-ever five -star General, the equivalent of a British Field Marshal.

Churchill called Marshall 'the organiser of victory' and he was roundly lauded even by his peers in America. On V.E. Day in America, Secretary of War Henry Stimson gathered together a group of leading generals and politicians before summoning Marshall, When Marshall arrived, he was told by Stimson, *'I have never seen a task of such magnitude performed by a man. I have seen a great many soldiers in my lifetime and you, Sir, are the finest soldier I have ever known.'*

With the war in Europe done, Marshall turned all his attention to planning the invasion of Japan. He had known about the atomic bomb project since 1941 and when it was suggested to use the weapon as an alternative to invasion, Marshall insisted it was a political and not a military question. He told. Assistant Secretary of War John McCloy, *'Don't ask me to make the decision.'*

He later said, 'The bomb stopped the war. Therefore, it was justifiable. I think it was very wise to use it.' However he took no pleasure in its use. The day after Hiroshima, he warned fellow generals against *'too much gratification over our success, because it undoubtedly involved a large number of Japanese casualties.'*

Marshall resigned as army Chief of Staff in 1945. In December that year, he was despatched to China by President Truman to try and broker peace between the Nationalist and Communist Armies there. His mission was a failure. Marshall's true passion now was to help Europe to recover from the Second World War. The European Recovery Program – which soon became known as The Marshall Plan – was intended to assist in the rebuilding of European society, infrastructure and national economies. In total, the U.S. donated over $13 billion in five years. It was, Churchill said, *'the most unsordid act in history.'* Marshall found himself Time magazine's Man of The Year in 1947 and, in 1953 he was awarded the Nobel Peace Prize.

Marshall resigned from the U.S. State Department in 1949 on the grounds of poor health but was dragged back to work as Secretary of Defense in September 1950 as the Korean War flared up. He served for one year. Despite being a true American hero, founder of the modern American Army and one of the founding fathers of NATO (and Truman hailing him as *'the greatest living American'*), Marshall was in 1951 being targeted by the notorious U.S. Senator Joseph McCarthy for allegedly being a tool of the Soviets and the Red Chinese. Marshall, according to McCarthy, was part of *'a conspiracy on a scale so immense as to dwarf any previous such venture in the history of man.'* McCarthy's absurd attack was not widely agreed with, but it added to Marshall's growing sense of alienation from politics and he finally retired in September 1951.

Marshall died on October 16th 1959. He was 78 years old and left no memoirs.

'Nice chap, no General'
General Montgomery

"I hate war as only a soldier who has lived it can, only as one who has seen its brutality, its stupidity.'
Eisenhower

EISENHOWER - THE SPEARHEAD

It's one of the enjoyable ironies of the Second World War that the General who did so much to defeat the Nazi threat was himself of German descent – on both sides of his family.

Dwight David Eisenhower was born into a strictly religious family in Denison Texas on October 14th 1890. He was the third of seven brothers – all of whom were nicknamed Ike. Dwight was 'Little Ike' to his family. Although a qualified engineer, his father had been reduced to washing down steam locomotives for a pittance and the family lived in a tumbledown shack. When he was a toddler the family moved from Texas to Abilene, Kansas in search of better work. They had just $24 to their name, but finally made a success of it in Kansas, although not before Eisenhower was bullied by other children for having to wear hand-me-downs and his mother's old shoes.

As he grew up, Eisenhower enjoyed a lot of outdoor sports including hunting and fishing, and also developed the dubious skills of a serious card shark – a trade taught to him by a old homeless man camping on the banks of a nearby river.

Eisenhower first considered joining the Naval Academy but finally settled on West Point instead. His mother was opposed to the idea, as she thought that war was 'rather wicked', but didn't stop him. She dutifully took him to the station, saw him off and then returned and wept bitterly. It was the only time her family had ever seen her cry.

Eisenhower found West Point difficult. He bridled against the many seemingly pointless regulations and traditions and could only prove himself an average student at the very best. His teachers never thought he would amount to much of an officer, as he took too much delight in playing practical jokes. He did however excel at both sport (until sustaining a very serious sports injury) and fleecing his fellow cadets in card games for significant sums of money. He graduated in 1915.

1916 saw Eisenhower – now a 2nd Lieutenant - stationed in Texas, where he met and later proposed to Mamie Geneva Doud, a young girl from an exceptionally wealthy family. They married in July 1916 and would later have two sons. Their first Doud Dwight 'Icky' Eisenhower tragically died of scarlet fever aged just 3. For the rest of his life, Eisenhower would send Mamie flowers on Icky's birthday.

When America entered the Great War, Eisenhower requested to be posted to Europe but instead ended up a temporary Lieutenant Colonel attached to America's first Tank Corps, which drove around the Gettysburg battlefield on manoeuvres a lot but which never got to see actual combat before the war ended.

Post war, Eisenhower was promoted to Major and stayed with the tanks. He and other up and coming tank specialists - including George S. Patton - developed their own theories of lightning warfare using tanks which paralleled the tactics the Germans would use in the Blitzkrieg in 1940. The High Command were not

Thos. E.
Stephens

impressed, believing that tanks were only good to provide close-in support for slow moving infantry, and when Eisenhower carried on championing his own ideas, he was threatened with court martial. He shut up.

After Pearl Harbor, Eisenhower was attached to the General Staff in Washington at the rank of Brigadier General. He became assistant Chief of Staff in charge of the new Operations Division under Chief of Staff General George C. Marshall, who had spotted Eisenhower's talent and had marked him for promotion. In June 1942, Eisenhower was despatched to England to take up the post of Commanding General, European Theater of Operations. The British were – at least initially, none too impressed, Brooke wrote of him in his diary that he was *'hopeless. He submerges himself in politics and neglects his military duties, partly ... because he knows little if anything about military matters.'*

In November 1942, Eisenhower was also appointed Supreme Commander Allied Expeditionary Force of the North African Theatre of Operations. Now he took command of the British territory of Gibraltar and there, in deep underground caverns, worked to plan Operation Torch – the Allied invasion of North Africa. Torch would prove a valuable learning experience for Eisenhower, both in terms of tactics and man management. From Operation Torch, Eisenhower moved on to oversee the invasion of Sicily and then Italy. Even with three major successful assaults behind him, Eisenhower was still stunned to discover that it was he – and not Marshall – whom Roosevelt had selected to take charge of the invasion of Europe as Supreme Allied Commander of the Allied Expeditionary Force. He announced to his wife in something of a daze.

'I'm going to command the whole shebang!'

Eisenhower was not certain that D-Day would be a success. He did, in fact, prepare a speech for the eventuality that it would fail. In part, it read:

'Our landings in the Cherbourg-Havre area have failed to gain a satisfactory foothold and I have withdrawn the troops. My decision to attack at this time and place was based on the best information available. The troops, the air and the Navy did all that bravery and devotion to duty could do. If any blame or fault attaches to the attempt, it is mine alone.'

The public never got to hear the speech. D-Day worked, and it worked magnificently.

In December 1944, Eisenhower was promoted to General of the Army, a rank equivalent to the British Field Marshal. He was also Time magazine's 'Man of the Year'. Throughout 1944 and 1945 he remained in overall command of the Allied liberation effort, trying to balance the competing demands of Montgomery and Bradley. After victory, Eisenhower briefly became the Military Governor of the U.S. Occupation Zone in Germany. He was generally benevolent to the enemy, shipping in hundreds of thousand tonnes of food for a German population nearing starvation and encouraging fraternisation between the occupying troops and the German people. At the same time, he went hard after the true Nazis, insisting on rigorous photographic evidence be taken of the concentration camps for use at the Nuremberg War Crimes Trials. By November 1945, Eisenhower was back in America taking over the post of Chief of Staff of the Army from George Marshall.

Eisenhower had always believed that politics and the military should not be combined. However, influential people behind the scenes were now looking at him and seeing a future president. Eisenhower initially resisted, saying that he didn't want to stand for any political office whether it be 'dogcatcher (or) Grand High Supreme King of the Universe'. He categorically stated: 'life-long professional soldiers, in the absence of some obvious and overriding reason, (should) abstain from seeking high political office'.

On January 20th 1953, having finally given in to the pressure, Eisenhower became the 34th President of the United States. Eisenhower campaigned on ending the Korean War, keeping the communists in check and ending Washington corruption. He won by a landslide. He would stand and win again in 1956.

Behind the scenes in the White House, Eisenhower enjoyed painting in oils and reading the potboiler westerns of Zane Grey. He also became a keen golfer and set up a putting green on the lawns of the White House, where he waged a constant and ill-tempered war against the squirrels who kept putting him off his game. At night, he loved to sit in front of the TV watching westerns while eating TV dinners off a tray.

He left office in 1961 and he and Mamie returned to their farm on the Gettysburg Battlefield. Eisenhower was in increasingly frail health now. Eisenhower died of heart failure, aged 78, on March 28th 1969. His last words were,' *I want to go; God take me.'* After a funeral in Washington, his body was put aboard a train for his childhood home of Abilene, Kansas. He was laid to rest in the grounds of his own Presidential Library in a humble $80 casket, in the uniform of a General. He was buried next to his three year old son Doud, lost in 1921. Mamie joined him after her death in 1979.

CLOCKWISE FROM TOP LEFT: 1916: Mamie Eisenhower and Dwight D. Eisenhower on front steps of St. Louis Hall, San Antonio, Texas; 15TH MAY 1944: Eisenhower, Churchill and LTG Omar Bradley shooting the M1 Carbine during preparations for Operation Overlord; 7TH MAY 1945: Eisenhower and Air Chief Marshal Sir Arthur Tedder, RAF, address the World shortly after Germany's unconditional surrender, at Rheims, France; 5TH JUNE 1944: Eisenhower gives the order of the Day. 'Full victory-nothing less' to paratroopers in England, just before they board their airplanes to participate in the first assault in the invasion; 1944: Eisenhower in his jeep in the American sector during the liberation of Lower Normandy